IN OUR TIME:
THE FLOWERING OF JEWISH-CATHOLIC DIALOGUE

Studies in Judaism and Christianity

Exploration of Issues in the
Contemporary Dialogue Between
Christians and Jews

Editor in Chief for
Stimulus Books
Helga Croner

Editors
Lawrence Boadt, C.S.P.
Helga Croner
Leon Klenicki
John Koenig
Kevin A. Lynch, C.S.P.

 A STIMULUS BOOK

IN OUR TIME

The Flowering of Jewish-Catholic Dialogue

Eugene J. Fisher and Leon Klenicki
Editors

With an Annotated Bibliography
by Eugene J. Fisher

A STIMULUS BOOK

Paulist Press ■ New York ■ Mahwah, N.J.

Library of Congress Cataloging-in-Publication Data

In our time: the flowering of Jewish-Catholic dialogue/edited by Eugene Fisher and Leon Klenicki.
    p. cm.—(Studies in Judaism and Christianity) (A Stimulus book)
    ISBN 0-8091-3196-X
    1. Catholic Church—Relations—Judaism—Sources. 2. Judaism—Relations—Catholic Church—Sources. 3. Catholic Church—Doctrines—History—20th century—Sources. 4. Judaism—Relations—Christianity—1945—Bibliography. 5. Christianity and other religions—Judaism—1945- —Bibliography.
    I. Klenicki, Leon. II. Fisher, Eugene, 1943- . III. Series.
    BM535.I483   1990
    261.2'6—dc20
                                      90-42678
                                          CIP

Published by Paulist Press
997 Macarthur Boulevard
Mahwah, New Jersey 07430

Printed and bound in the United States of America

Contents

I. OFFICIAL ROMAN CATHOLIC TEACHING ON JEWS AND JUDAISM

1. Official Roman Catholic Teaching on Jews and Judaism:
   Commentary and Context
   Eugene J. Fisher 3

2. Appendix: The Development of a Tradition 19

II. VATICAN DOCUMENTS ON CATHOLIC-JEWISH RELATIONS

1. Declaration on the Relationship of the Church to Non-
   Christian Religions [*Nostra Aetate* (no. 4) (October 28, 1965)]
   Ecumenical Council Vatican II 27

2. Guidelines and Suggestions for Implementing the Conciliar
   Declaration *Nostra Aetate* (no. 4) [December 1, 1974]
   Vatican Commission for Religious Relations with the Jews ... 29

3. Notes on the Correct Way to Present the Jews and Judaism in
   Preaching and Catechesis in the Roman Catholic Church
   [June 24, 1985]
   Vatican Commission for Religious Relations with the Jews ... 38

III. STATEMENTS ON CATHOLIC-JEWISH RELATIONS

1. A Note for the Presentation of the Document of the
   Commission for Religious Relations with the Jews [Notes on

the Correct Way to Present the Jews and Judaism in
Preaching and Catechesis in the Roman Catholic Church]
Jorge Mejia   53

2. Within Context: Guidelines for the Catechetical Presentation
of Jews and Judaism in the New Testament [1986]
Secretariat for Catholic-Jewish Relations, NCCB;
Adult Education Department, USCC; Interfaith Affairs
Department, ADL   59

IV. FROM ARGUMENT TO DIALOGUE:
NOSTRA AETATE TWENTY-FIVE YEARS LATER

From Argument to Dialogue: *Nostra Aetate* Twenty-Five
Years Later
Leon Klenicki   77

V. A NEW MATURITY IN
CHRISTIAN-JEWISH DIALOGUE

A New Maturity in Christian-Jewish Dialogue: An Annotated
Bibliography 1975–1989
Eugene J. Fisher   107

    1. Documenting the Dialogue
    2. The New Testament and Judaism
    3. The Trial of Jesus
    4. The Relationship between the Scriptures
    5. The Patristic Period
    6. The Medieval Period and the Reformation
    7. The Modern Period: Jews and Christians in America
    8. Mission and Witness Reconsidered
    9. Toward a Christian Theology of Judaism
   10. Jewish Responses to Christianity
   11. Liturgy, Spirituality and Catechetics
   12. The Holocaust and Christian-Jewish Relations
   13. Muslim-Jewish-Christian Relations

ACKNOWLEDGMENT

The authors wish to acknowledge the cooperation of the Interfaith Affairs Department of the Anti-Defamation League of B'nai B'rith
and
the Secretariat for Ecumenical and Interreligious Affairs of the National Conference of Catholic Bishops in developing these materials.

I.
OFFICIAL ROMAN CATHOLIC TEACHING ON JEWS AND JUDAISM

1. Official Roman Catholic Teaching on Jews and Judaism: Commentary and Context

Eugene J. Fisher

INTRODUCTION: AN HISTORICAL *UNICUM*

The three documents included here constitute, remarkably, the entire corpus of universal Roman Catholic teaching concerning the church's attitude toward Jews and Judaism since the close of the apostolic age. This is not to claim that nothing was said by popes or ecumenical councils during the intervening nineteen centuries. Much was said. Nor is it to claim that what was said, unlike the present documents, was entirely positive in intent or in its effects on Jews living within the confines of Christendom.

Much was said in papal and conciliar decrees about Jews and about Judaism. But the statements, though bearing heavily on the lives of Jews, were disciplinary in character, not doctrinal. They range in time from the somewhat grudgingly protectionist legislation of Gregory the Great, made into lasting canon law by inclusion in Gratian's *Decretum* and the "Constitution for the Jews" (*Sicut Judaeis non*) which was reaffirmed by the popes throughout the Middle Ages and into the modern era, to the more negative decrees of the Fourth Lateran Council (1215), which signalled the institution of such dubious measures as the creation of ghettos (a level of repression unknown for the first millennium of Jewish-Christian interaction in Europe). Though often negative, the point of those official Catholic statements was not to determine the *meaning* of Judaism from the point of view of Catholic doctrine, but rather to define the position of Jews within Christian society.[1]

The importance of this seemingly technical detail cannot be overestimated. Because of it, Cardinal Johannes Willebrands, president of the Pontifical Council for Religious Relations with the Jews, was able to call the first of the three documents included here "an absolute *unicum*" in the history of the church. "Never before," he stated, "has a systematic, positive, comprehensive, careful and daring presentation of Jews and Judaism been made in the church."[2]

It may also be said that the reason that neither popes nor councils, over the centuries, felt called upon to decree officially on the church's doctrinal position with regard to Judaism was most likely that no one questioned the negative portrait of the Jewish religion drawn by the church fathers in the early centuries. With no Christians rising to question the distorted image of Judaism provided in the patristic texts, this ancient Christian "teaching of contempt" did not have to be officially defined but was simply presumed by just about all Christian thinkers until the present century.

The three statements presented here, then, represent the sum and substance of official church teaching concerning Jews and Judaism on the universal level. For all practical purposes they *are,* taken together, the definitive utterance of Catholic tradition, the *magisterium* on the subject universally binding on the presentation of the Catholic faith by catechists and homilists alike.

Yet, these statements, while they have no true doctrinal precedents in church history, do have a wider context in the statements of the popes and of local churches since the Second Vatican Council. In this commentary, then, we shall rely on these resources, especially the many reflections of Pope John Paul II and, in our own context, the implementing statements of the U.S. National Conference of Catholic Bishops, to provide insights into and possible applications of their remarkable teachings.

A. THE DOCUMENTS: BRIEF COMMENTARIES

The three documents included here are:

1. *Nostra Aetate, No. 4.*
Issued on October 28, 1965, by Pope John Paul VI and 2,221 bishops from around the world, this is the key statement with regard to Catholic-Jewish Relations of the Second Vatican Council. The full docu-

ment, entitled "Declaration on the Relationship of the Church to Non-Christian Religions," dealt positively also with other major world religions, such as Islam, Buddhism, and Hinduism. According to Cardinal Willebrands, who worked on the document during the council, "the document (*Nostra Aetate*) gives pride of place, both in dignity and in affection, to Judaism, the olive branch onto which Christianity was grafted (Rom 11:17–24)."[3] Willebrands aptly summarizes the council's message, repeated also in the council's major Constitution on the Church in the Modern World (*Lumen Gentium,* No. 16) in a single sentence: "As the church ponders the mystery of the salvation of all mankind in Christ, she is able to affirm the deep spiritual bond between Jews and Christians within God's loving plan for the redemption of the world."[4]

What a startling, some would even say revelatory, statement that was when it came out in 1965! It is, I would submit, no less challenging for us today. To see the church as not alone in the unfolding and proclamation of the divine mysteries! To view another religion, and one traditionally pilloried by Christians in the most negative fashion ("legalistic," "carnal," "usurious," "spiritually blind," "bloodthirsty," etc.) as the church's spiritual partner *within* God's redemptive design! To use the sacred terminology normally reserved for the sacraments themselves ("mystery of salvation," "spiritual bond") to describe the relationship today between the church and the Jewish people!

Given the long, tragic centuries of oppression and persecution, of Crusading violence and Inquisitional (at least in Spain) torture, of exile and forced baptism, of ghettos and pogroms, "daring" may be an understatement for what those 2,221 bishops, sitting in solemn council, achieved, as Father Thomas Stransky has noted, "with only fifteen long Latin sentences."[5]

Briefly, *Nostra Aetate* "acknowledges" the church's indebtedness to Judaism, in which "the beginnings of her (the church's) faith and her election are already found." Far from replacing or superseding Jewish faith, Christians are "included in the patriarch's (Abraham's) call."

Nor is this Christian indebtedness simply a thing of the past, as if Judaism's sole role was exhausted in foreshadowing Christianity. Using the vibrant imagery of St. Paul's letter to the Romans (11:17–24), in which the "root" is biblical Israel and the "wild olive branches" are the Gentiles, the council significantly puts in the present tense the statement that the church cannot "forget that she draws sustenance from the root of that good olive tree."

Nostra Aetate also resolved a long-standing dispute among biblical translators by translating in the present tense a key passage of Romans 9:4–5, in which St. Paul speaks of the Jewish people, even after the coming of Christ, as those "who have the adoption as sons, and the glory and the covenant and the legislation and the worship and the promise." In the Greek, this passage has no verb, so it has been, before the council, possible for polemically-minded translators to render it in the past tense: "theirs *were* the adoption," etc., implying that God's covenant with the Jewish people had been abrogated in favor of "the Christian dispensation" with the coming of Christ.

The problem with this negative, abrogationist translation, biblically, is that the ruling verb, *eisin,* in a preceding passage, is in the present tense so it ought, by New Testament grammar, to have been translated in the present all along, as the council correctly (and definitively) deduced.

Again, the difference may appear to be a small technical one, as with the fact noted above that the Second Vatican Council, approaching the issue of Catholic-Jewish relations, had no previous official tradition in church teaching to rule on. But again, in such matters, the small detail is often the crucial one. Though overlooked by most commentators on the declaration, this single act of properly translating Paul's letter to the Romans according to the apostle's own evident intent overturned volumes of popular-level anti-Jewish polemics.

For if God's covenant and legislation (what used to be called the "Old Law," but is best rendered as "Torah"—God's divine teaching for the Jews) remains valid for the Jews, today no less than in biblical times, then the Jews cannot validly be called "unfaithful" or "blind" or "legalistic" in remaining faithful to it. Rather, Jews practicing Judaism must be honored, indeed revered by Christians precisely for their faithfulness. Only in this way can Christians honor and revere God's faithfulness to the divine promises, whether those made to Jews or, through Christ, to the world. As St. Paul knew and the council rediscovered, if God has not been faithful to the Jews, on what basis can we claim that God will be faithful to that which is revealed to us in Christ?

Noting without comment the indisputable historical fact that "Jews in large number" did not "accept the gospel" and some "opposed" it, the council quite logically concluded with St. Paul that even though not baptised "the Jews still remain most dear to God because of their fathers, for God does not repent of the gifts he makes nor of the calls He issues (cf. Rom 11:28–29)."

Noting again as historical fact that certain "authorities of the Jews and those who followed their lead pressed for the death of Christ (cf. Jn 19:6)," the council denounced any collective guilt on "the Jews then living," much less on "the Jews of today" for Christ's death.

This historic condemnation of the ancient "deicide" (Christ-killer) charge against the Jews, a canard which caused so much destruction in the past, prefaces the second major (and equally often overlooked) official hermeneutic (point of biblical interpretation) in *Nostra Aetate, No. 4:* "The Jews should not be presented as repudiated or cursed by God, *as if such views followed from the holy scriptures.*"

This completes the hermeneutical circle begun with the present-tense translation of Romans 9:4–5. Since the entire structure of the old "teaching of contempt" was posited on the erroneous notion that God had "repudiated" the Jews because of their so-called failure to accept Jesus as "the Christ," one can no longer denigrate the Jewish people today using Christian theological premises.

Nostra Aetate, No. 4, together with the two implementing documents provided thus far by the Holy See, the 1974 *Guidelines* and the 1985 *Notes,* to be discussed below, remain the official expression of the *Magisterium* on the subject. While their multifaceted implications are still being worked out by Catholic theologians and bishops alike, it is worth noting that these are definitive in a certain sense of all that will follow in unfolding them. Speaking of the biblical points that we have here stressed, Bishop Jorge Mejia in 1978, then Secretary of the Vatican Commission, noted that "for what regards the points which touch on the interpretation of scripture, the Catholic teacher has here the true norm for reading scripture when it refers to Jews and Judaism."[6]

2. *Guidelines and Suggestions for Implementing the Conciliar Declaration, Nostra Aetate, No. 4.*

It took the Holy See's Commission for Religious Relations with the Jews nearly a decade to issue its initial document for *Nostra Aetate.* Presumably, this was to allow time for the dialogue to mature to the point where it could be written based upon experience rather than mere theory.

The chart, in the Appendix to this article, shows the interrelationships between *Nostra Aetate,* the *Guidelines* (1974) and the *Notes* (1985). In doing so, the chart concentrates on points that may have been considered only implicitly in *Nostra Aetate* but which have been made increasingly explicit as the work of implementing the council both in the church universal and in local communities has been carried out in the quarter-century since its promulgation.

The intent of the *Guidelines,* its introductory note states, is a practical one: "To give ideas (on) how to start on a local level . . . the movement of the universal church in dialogue with Judaism." Its four sections deal, in turn, with the nature of dialogue, Christian liturgy and education, and common social action. While it disclaims to be proposing "a Christian theology of Judaism," the *Guidelines* propositions do in fact contain much that is of theological value in the areas discussed.

In its Preamble, the *Guidelines* acknowledge what was obvious but unstated during the Second Vatican Council; namely, that *Nostra Aetate* "finds its historical setting in circumstances deeply affected by the memory of the persecution and massacre of Jews which took place in Europe just before and during the Second World War." Yet it will not be until the 1985 *Notes* that the Holy See will mandate the development of a catechesis of the *Shoah.*

On reflection, the reasons behind this reticence may become clear. In 1974, few Catholics even knew the word, "Holocaust," as it refers to the Nazis' systematic genocidal attack upon the Jewish people of Europe. Fewer still, even in the Jewish community, made use of the Hebrew term *Shoah,* which indicates a devastating and all-consuming wind, to refer to that massive tragedy. Indeed, it was not until the late 1970s that many Jewish survivors, perhaps emboldened by the popular T.V. miniseries on the Holocaust, were willing to come forth in public to speak of their searing experiences.

This period of silence, almost a generation long, on the part of the Jewish community with reference to the Holocaust, is a measure of the depth of the trauma they have suffered in this century: two-thirds of European Jewry murdered, one-third of the entire Jewish people. Put in American terms, it is as if the population of the entire East Coast had been massacred. Virtually every Jew in America lost relatives in the death camps of Nazi Europe, some very close, such as parents or cousins or sisters and brothers. It is just now, within the past decade, that they have begun to speak of it openly.

It is understandable, then, that the church, too, has preserved until recently its own reverential silence in the face of this *mysterium tremendum*[7] of evil and improbable Jewish hope, especially in view of the fact that, as Bishop James Malone, speaking as president of the National Conference of Catholic Bishops, put it so well, "Christians were numbered both among the executioners and the victims [of the death camps]. At one and the same time, Christians were both oppressor and oppressed."[8]

Even now, the church must search its language with extreme caution and ultimate humility before speaking of the *Shoah*. For it is the church's task to listen first to the Jewish witness before attempting its own. In a remarkable address to the tiny remnant of the once great Jewish community of Warsaw, Poland, in 1987, Pope John Paul II made very clear the primacy of the Jewish experience in this century:

> It was you (Jews) who suffered this terrible sacrifice of extermination. One might say that you suffered it also on behalf of those (the Polish Church) who were likewise to have been exterminated. . . . Today, this nation of Israel has become a loud warning voice for all humanity. More than anyone else, it is precisely you who have become this saving warning. In this sense you continue your particular vocation, showing yourselves to be still the heirs of that election to which God is faithful. This is your mission in the contemporary world . . . and in the church, peoples and nations feel united to you in this mission.[9]

The saving witness to the crucial events of this century, and their proper interpretation, belongs to the Jewish people. The church's mission today is to listen, to affirm, and to unite its voice to that of the Jews.

After summarizing the Second Vatican Council's teaching and repeating its condemnation of anti-Semitism, the *Guidelines* offer a positive definition of dialogue regarding "the fundamental convictions of Judaism and of Christianity." Far from the polemical and proselytizing motivations that marred the medieval disputations, the *Guidelines* call for "a great openness of spirit and diffidence with respect to one's own prejudices." To be in dialogue means that each partner is the expert in what he or she believes: "Dialogue demands respect for the other as he is; above all, respect for his faith and religious convictions."

This is an important admonition. For centuries, beginning as early as Justin Martyr's so-called "Dialogue" (really, a polemic) with Trypho, Christian teachers have tended to ascribe to Judaism beliefs and practices that are alien to Jewish tradition, such as "legalism," "carnality," and "religious hypocrisy." The low point in this sad history of malicious projection appeared as early as the thirteenth century, with the popular belief that Jews sought to murder Christian children in order to use their blood to make the Passover bread. In the fourteenth century, this was embellished with the curious notion that Jews had caused the Black Plague by poisoning the wells (from which, as the popes pointed out in the period, they themselves drank!).

Though repeatedly condemned by the papacy over the centuries, such "blood libel" and ancillary charges continued to be made—and even worse, widely believed—well into the present century. They were a central feature of Nazi propaganda and can still be found in neo-Nazi and other hate literature, even in this country. They are embedded as well in some of our greatest literature, such as the figure of the moneylender in Shakespeare's *The Merchant of Venice,* who demands his pound of flesh from a debtor, and in the figure of Fagin who, in *Oliver Twist,* systematically corrupts young boys. Educators and parents should be aware that the world our children will inherit, as well as the very language we speak, is laced with remnants of the Western world's anti-Semitic past. Some people still say "to Jew someone down" when they mean "to bargain," and lovingly plant "Wandering Jews" in their gardens.

The *Guidelines'* section on dialogue notes as well that "the witness of Catholics to Jesus Christ" in whatever circumstances, is limited by the need to maintain "the strictest respect for religious liberty." In 1977, in a meeting in Venice of the International Catholic-Jewish Liaison Committee, Catholic theologian Tommaso Federici drew out the implications of this mandate, based upon the nature of faith as God's free gift calling for the human person's free response. While the church's witness is, as it has always been, universal and without exception, "attempts to set up organizations of any sort, particularly educational or welfare organizations, for the 'conversion' of Jews must be rejected" by Catholics. "Simultaneously," Federici concludes, "what the Jews have to say" to *us* "must be listened to."[10] Otherwise, we risk bearing false witness of and to the Jewish people who were and are God's chosen.

With regard to the *liturgy,* the *Guidelines* begin to tackle one of the thorniest problems of contemporary Christian theology: how to deal with the promise-fulfillment theme that is central to our liturgical selection of readings from the sacred scriptures. Acknowledging the indebtedness of Christian liturgy to Jewish liturgy and the existing links between the two sacred worship traditions, the *Guidelines* first note that there is much in the Hebrew scriptures that "retains its own perpetual value (cf. *Dei Verbum,* 14–15)" and "has not been cancelled by the later interpretation of the New Testament." The *Guidelines* do not define precisely the *extent* of this "whatever" in the Hebrew Bible that retains its spiritual integrity even after the coming of Christ. One would presume it to be extensive, since it was God's revelation before Christ and therefore cannot be deemed cancelled without demeaning the integrity of God's word. Conceivably, the entire corpus of the Hebrew scriptures could be included in this "whatever," but neither *Dei Verbum,* 16 nor the *Guidelines* make this explicit.

The *Guidelines* do, however, offer a most helpful, if somewhat awkwardly phrased, basis for a positive theology of "the continuity of our faith with that of the earlier covenant," by stating that Christians "believe that these promises were fulfilled with the first coming of Christ" but have not yet achieved their "perfect fulfillment." This "unfulfilled" aspect of the church's proclamation of Christ (also called the "eschatological caveat" in theological terminology) will become the central feature of the Commission's reflections on the "relations between" the Testaments (and therefore the covenants the books embody) in its 1985 *Notes*.

Here, let it suffice to say what the *Guidelines* directly imply. First, it is no longer valid for Catholics to argue that we "have" what Jews only "await," namely, the messiah. The messianic age, the reign of God, is truly in our midst through Christ, but it is not yet complete. We, no less than the Jews, await that fullness of time. The Jews, in short, have not been wrong to insist on waiting still for their messiah. In doing so, it may be said, the Jews witness to the "not yet" aspect of the good news.

It is not, then, that we Christians say "Yes" to God's reign, while Jews say "No" to it. Jews no less than Christians proclaim with full integrity the kingdom of God and we Christians must revere them for it and be willing to stand by their side in that proclamation. This vision of a joint witness to God's reign, as we shall see, permeates the 1985 *Notes* and is, perhaps, what lies behind the *Guidelines'* cautious and sensitive call for joint prayer and common social action "in the spirit of the prophets" with respect to "the struggle for peace and justice."

The *Guidelines'* section on Catholic education again delineates themes that will be developed in greater detail in the 1985 statement. Noting the rich spiritual vitality of Judaism in New Testament times, the *Guidelines* affirm that Jewish tradition has continued to be "rich in religious values" down to the present. Like the Hebrew scriptures, ongoing Jewish tradition is a living reality, not a past one, its contribution to sacred history by no means exhausted in giving birth to Christianity. It maintains its own integrity that is not fully encompassed in its relationship with Christianity, historically or spiritually, even though that particular aspect of Judaism quite naturally is the one that most deeply attracts Christians to it.

Though the *Guidelines* stress the "profoundly new character" of God's revelation in Christ, they preclude any catechesis which would set the one against the other. Jesus' law of love, the *Guidelines* note, is no more and no less than the Torah's own law of love. Jesus simply (and most aptly) cites Deuteronomy 6:5 ("Love God with your whole heart," etc.) and Leviticus 19:18 ("Love your neighbor as yourself") when asked to summarize the inner meaning of the commandments. It is a summary similar to that given by rabbinic tradition as well. Indeed, one can find a version of the golden rule in the Talmud ascribed to the great Pharisaic sage Hillel who lived in the century *before* Christ.

So the relationship between Judaism and Christianity can never accurately be characterized in negative terms. Like the relationship between the scriptures, to which the *Guidelines* refer, citing from *Dei Verbum* 16, the relationship is best understood as a positive, reciprocal one with each, insofar as they touch on the same spiritual realities, most often serving to illuminate each other, rather than vying against one another in some sort of childish religious turf war. Jews and Christians, the *Guidelines* affirm, have much to learn from one another, and much too much to do together in and for the world to continue the petty games of theological polemics that have so scarred our mutual, too often tragic past.

3. *Notes on the Correct Way to Present the Jews and Judaism in Preaching and Catechesis* (June 24, 1985).

The Italian word here translated as "notes" is *sussidi,* which can also mean "aids" or "helps." The tentative character of this title should not mask the authoritative nature of the document as a teaching of the Holy See addressed to the whole church and binding on it. Rather, it refers to the fact that we are, even a quarter of a century into the historic dialogue with the Jewish people, far from knowing enough about Judaism and about our own faith tradition in relation to Judaism, to say at this stage that we can present any definitive or final word on the subject. We are still striving to articulate the proper questions, much less provide "the" answers to them.

A small example may be found in the document's first footnote, which explains why it continues to use the term "Old Testament," even though some may misconstrue the term to mean "out-of-date" or "outworn," as if God's revelation could ever become "old" in that pejorative sense. A little over a year after the issuance of the *Notes* on June 24, 1985, Pope John Paul II himself used the terms "Hebrew scriptures" and "Christian scriptures,"[11] as he has done since then. What seemed to the Commission in 1985 as a step whose time had not yet matured was, by 1986, already at least a valid option for Christians to use.

Another little detail may illustrate the extraordinary sensitivity with which the Holy See approaches this subject, which it considers not marginal but essential to church teaching. The date of issuance, June 24, was not accidental. That was the feast of St. John the Baptist. It was chosen, I was told, because he is a "Jewish saint," that is, not a "Christian" (since he died before Jesus). This was a small, but very telling reminder, to those who might need it, that Jews do not have to be baptized into the church in order to be "saved."

This point was made very sharply by Bishop Jorge Mejia of the Commission in introducing the text that day. In a paper published simultaneously with the document itself in *L'Osservatore Romano,* Mejia commented that while the statement affirms "the centrality of Christ and his unique value in the economy of salvation, clearly this does not mean, however, that the Jews cannot and should not have salvific gifts from their own teachings. Of course, they may and should do so."[12]

Mejia's commentary, I believe, is important for a proper understanding of the *Notes.* Published with the text, it guides the reader on the *Notes'* intent and focus, responding, at the same time, to many Jewish concerns raised, among others, by my colleague, Rabbi Klenicki.

The most difficult portion of the text is its second section on "relations" between the Testaments. This section, as has been pointed out, picks up the highly complex themes of typology and promise/fulfillment introduced by the Commission in 1974. Calling typology "the sign of a problem unresolved," it opens up for Catholic reflection an entire area of theology that one had thought a closed and simple matter.

Before the Second Vatican Council, most Christians thought the relationship between the Hebrew and Christian scriptures a relatively simple affair: the latter "perfected" or subsumed the former where they were perceived to agree, and abrogated or replaced it where they appeared to be in disagreement. Thus, "Old" Testament figures, events and even teachings were seen as mere "types" or "shadows" of the later revelation.

The *Notes* list several ways in which the tradition of Christian typological reading of the Hebrew scriptures may be understood to remain valid today. But as Bishop Mejia comments, the *Notes* view typology as only one way of reading the scriptures. "Other possible ways of reading the Old Testament in relation to the New are not excluded," Mejia comments.[13] One example is of course the Way (*halakhah*) of Jewish tradition, from which Christians themselves can profit "discerningly" (II, 7).

Further, the *Notes* place the whole question of typology and fulfillment in their larger, eschatological context, thus in a very real sense relativizing these ancient Christian traditions by orienting them to their

proper end in the "final consummation" of the coming of God's reign at
the end of time.

In this sense, Mejia comments, the *Notes* open up a startling new
angle on the church's own self-understanding. Both the New Testament
and the church's own sacraments are, "with respect to the last things,"
typological themselves, no less than are the Hebrew scriptures and Rabbinic Judaism. Neither the church nor the Jewish people, the *Notes*
maintain, exist for themselves but are called to sense God's ultimate
purpose. Rather than asking "Who is right? They or We?" the *Notes* set
Catholic-Jewish dialogue in a larger frame of "comparable hope."

In 1988, the National Conference of Catholic Bishops' Committee
on the Liturgy issued guidelines for preachers based upon the *Notes*. With
respect to the fulfillment theme of Advent, the bishops' guidelines state:

> This truth needs to be framed very carefully. Christians believe that
> Jesus is the promised Messiah who has come (Luke 4:22), but also
> know that his messianic kingdom is not yet fully realized. . . . While the
> biblical prophecies of an age of universal *Shalom* are "fulfilled" (i.e.,
> irreversibly inaugurated) in Christ's coming, that fulfillment is not yet
> completely worked out in each person's life or perfected in the world at
> large. It is the mission of the Church to prepare the world for the full
> flowering of God's Reign, which is, but is "not yet." Both the Christian
> "Our Father" and the Jewish *Kaddish* exemplify this message. Both
> Christianity and Judaism seal their worship with a common hope:
> "Thy kingdom come!" With the Jewish people, we await the complete
> realization of the messianic age.[14]

This renewed Catholic vision of Jews and Christians standing together to work for and await God's reign goes, as the *Notes* say, "beyond
simple dialogue." It reminds both communities that there is something
far more important than merely "being right," as if truth were a limited
and packageable commodity that one can possess at the expense of another. Rather, God possesses us all. That is the essence of the truth both
traditions proclaim. Neither is subsumed into the other. Both, however,
are quite properly consumed by this most sacred task.

This section also points to an ongoing difficulty in the dialogue. Jews
and Christians, while having much of their religious vocabulary in common, since both derive from the same source, biblical Israel, do not
always mean the same things when they use the same terms. Even basic
words such as "messiah," "redemption," and "salvation" have very different meanings in the two communities. Thus, for a Christian to say to

Jews that Jesus is "your messiah" in whom alone "you can be saved" is to make a statement which Jews find utterly incomprehensible. So, too, is it incomprehensible to Christians for Jews to tell them that belief in the Trinity means that Christians do not believe in the Oneness of God. In both cases the key terms are simply not understood in the same way by the two traditions. In both, one may say, one side has presented an answer to which the other does not have the corresponding question.

Two millennia of separate, though in many ways intertwined development lie behind these different usages of key terms, and the development of other terms unique to each. Neither side of the dialogue may presume to understand the other tradition to the point of being able to sit in judgment upon it. The only truly prophetic critique is self-critique. And, as the *Notes* emphasize, we Christians have all too much of which to repent when it comes to our treatment of the Jewish people over the ages.

The third and fourth sections of the *Notes* go into very practical details on understanding how the New Testament is to be interpreted with respect to Jews and Judaism. The notion that Jesus in his life and teachings somehow opposed Judaism and Jewish law is thoroughly debunked. Jesus remained a faithful, observant Jew all his life, though offering some unique insights into the Jewish tradition.

Jesus shared many central teachings with the Pharisees; in fact, most especially those beliefs (resurrection of the body, praying to God as Father, the law of love, etc.) which most clearly distinguished Pharisaic beliefs and practices from those of other Jewish groups of the period. Nor are the Pharisees mentioned in the gospels as being involved in Jesus' death, but rather seek to warn him of the plot against his life (Lk 13:31). So to present the Pharisees as the foils of the Jesus story (playing the villains to Jesus as hero) is to seriously misrepresent the gospel narratives. Jesus argues with the Pharisees over points of Jewish Law because he shares their concern for its observance and proper understanding. One does not spend so much time debating with those one holds in contempt, but rather with those one cares about most deeply.

The *Notes* also point out that the gospels were set down only at the end of the first century, after the split between the growing rabbinic and Jesus movements had already occurred. So the sense of conflict it portrays often reflects not a conflict between Jesus and his fellow Jews, but between the later Jewish and Christian communities, a conflict we need not perpetuate today but rather ought to seek to heal.

While *some* Jews were historically involved in Jesus' death, so were *some* Romans, chiefly Pilate, as our Creeds attest. Pilate was a vicious tyrant who crucified so many Jews ("by the hundreds," one ancient commentator puts it) that he was finally recalled by Rome for excessive brutality. So there can be no question of collective Jewish responsibility for Jesus' death, either then or now. Christians must look to their own sins, not to others', for this responsibility. In the United States, the previously mentioned document of the Bishops' Committee on the Liturgy, *God's Mercy,* and a statement of the NCCB Committee for Ecumenical and Interreligious Affairs, *Criteria for the Evaluation of Dramatizations of the Passion* (USCC Publication No. 211-X, 1988) draw out the implications of the *Notes* for local parishes and classrooms. The latter document will be especially helpful in dioceses and parishes where Passion Plays are put on, or in classes in Catholic schools.

The final section of the *Notes* is in a way a schema for a future document. It deals with "Judaism and Christianity in History," encapsulating two millennia in five brief paragraphs. Its acknowledgement that "the history of Israel did not end in A.D. 70" (citing the 1974 *Guidelines*) is itself remarkable, since for many Christians it was the presumption that the history of Israel *did* end with the destruction of the Temple by Rome, and that thereafter it was the church, not the Jewish people that carried forward sacred history. This section, understanding post-New Testament Jewish history as an extension of biblical history, acknowledges the ongoing integrity of Judaism as a "saving witness" in its own right in and for the world.

Whereas previous Christian polemics had interpreted the Temple's destruction and the Jewish people's dispersion (Diaspora) in negative terms as God's "curse" on the Jews for their alleged crime of deicide ("Christ-killers," Jews were often called), the *Notes* interpret the Diaspora in a positive fashion, as allowing Israel to carry throughout the world its own proper witness of its fidelity to God and of God's fidelity to Israel. Far from being subsumed into the Christian covenant, the Jewish covenant retains, as does Israel's Bible, its own integrity and perpetual value. The church recognizes this value and rejoices in it.

This sense of ongoing Jewish history as sacred history is linked by the *Notes* directly with the return in our own century of the Jewish people to the land of Israel, hinting at a theological appreciation not only for the "religious attachment" of the People of Israel to the land of Israel, but also at a positive theological understanding of the revival of a Jewish State (*medinat*) in the land (*eretz*) of Israel.

The *Notes* are careful, however, not to make more, theologically, of this link beyond affirming it as significant for our understanding of sacred history. "The permanence of Israel," the text states immediately after its consideration of the land and the State of Israel, "is a historic fact and a sign to be interpreted within God's design." The *Notes,* citing the 1975 "Statement on Catholic-Jewish Relations" of the U. S. Bishops' Conference (it is most unusual for a document of the Holy See to cite a statement of a local Conference), also contain a caution to Catholics not to make "their own any particular religious interpretation," but to see the State in "reference to the common principles of international law." The similar *caveat* to be found in the U. S. Bishops' statement is meant to tread warily with certain fundamentalist interpretations, both Protestant and Jewish, which would see in the State of Israel a direct "fulfillment" of the biblical promises in our time. As with the majority of the Jewish people, Catholic tradition would also approach such a claim very cautiously. It is too susceptible of abuse as a rationale for the policies of particular administrations. Catholicism, of course, saw such abuses with the "divine right of kings" theory and wishes to avoid them today.

Also significant in this section is the reference to Judaism's "continuous spiritual fecundity," in rabbinic, medieval and modern times. These, too, as well as the rebirth into hope of the Jewish people after the trauma of the *Shoah,* together form what the text means by "a sign to be interpreted within God's design." While it would perhaps be premature for the church to define more precisely the significance of that "sign," the *fact* that Judaism is a spiritual sign (one might say "sacrament" here) of the encounter with God is established as an essential element of Catholic catechesis. One can only look forward with eagerness to further statements from the Holy See's Commission.

NOTES

1. On Church texts relating to Jews and Judaism through the fifteenth century, see Edward A. Synan, *The Popes and the Jews in the Middle Ages* (New York: Macmillan, 1965).

2. Johannes Willebrands, "Vatican II and the Jews: Twenty Years Later," *Christian-Jewish Relations: A Documentary Survey* (London: Vol. 15, No. 1, March 1985) 16–17.

3. ———, "Preface" to *Fifteen Years of Catholic-Jewish Dialogue, 1970–1985* (Vatican City: Libreria Editrice Vaticana, 1985) vii. Hereinafter, *Fifteen Years.*

4. Ibid.

5. Thomas Stransky, C.S.P., "Focusing on Jewish-Catholic Relations," *Origins* (Washington, D. C.: Vol. 15, No. 5, 1985) 67.

6. *Fifteen Years,* 86.

7. See Eugene Fisher, "*Mysterium Tremendum:* Catholic Grapplings with the Holocaust and Its Theological Implications," *SIDIC* (Rome: Vol. 22, No. 1, 1989) 10–15. This is a special issue of the journal, containing a wealth of curriculum and resource references on the Holocaust for teachers and Catholic-Jewish dialogue groups.

8. Included in E. Fisher, et al., *Twenty Years of Jewish-Catholic Relations* (Mahwah: Paulist Press, 1986) 222–227. It is indicative of the leading role played by the U.S. dialogue that the very first set of guidelines issued anywhere in the world after the council was published by the NCCB Secretariat for Catholic-Jewish Relations in 1967.

9. In E. Fisher, ed., *John Paul II on the Holocaust* (Washington, D. C.: National Conference of Catholic Bishops, 1988) 8. For the full texts of the papal statements on Catholic-Jewish relations, with commentary, see Eugene Fisher and Leon Klenicki, eds., *Pope John Paul II on Jews and Judaism 1979–1986* (Washington/New York: NCCB and ADL, 1987).

10. Tommaso Federici, "Mission and Witness of the Church," *Fifteen Years, cit.,* 58–59.

11. John Paul II, "Address to the Jewish Community of Australia," in Fisher and Klenicki, *John Paul II,* 95.

12. *Fifteen Years,* 316.

13. Ibid., 316.

14. Bishops' Committee on the Liturgy, National Conference of Catholic Bishops, *God's Mercy Endures Forever: Guidelines on the Presentation of Jews and Judaism in Catholic Preaching* (Washington, D. C.: USCC Publication No. 247-O, September, 1988) 7–8.

Appendix:

The Development of a Tradition

The following chart* lists several areas in which the wording of the 1974 Vatican *Guidelines* and the more recent *Notes* have specifically clarified wording left "creatively vague" by the Second Vatican Council, thus determining how *Nostra Aetate* is today to be read. Many of these, it will be noted, are directly responsive to critiques made of *Nostra Aetate* and the 1974 *Guidelines* in the dialogue between Catholics and Jews sparked by the council. It is to be expected that the *Notes* will undergo a similar process of clarification through dialogue.

Nostra Aetate, 1965	*Vatican Guidelines, 1974*	*Notes for Preaching and Catechesis, 1985*
1) — "The Church decries hatred, persecutions and manifestations of anti-Semitism directed against Jews at any time and by anyone."	— "condemn, as opposed to the very spirit of Christianity, all forms of anti-Semitism and discrimination."	— "The urgency and importance of precise, objective and rigorously accurate teaching on Judaism for our faithful follows too from the danger of anti-Semitism, which is always ready to reappear under different guises" (I, 8). VI 26 reaffirms the condemnation of anti-Semitism.

* For the idea behind this chart, now much expanded, I am indebted to Jacqueline des Rochettes, "Evolution of a Vocabulary: A Sign of Hope?": *SIDIC* (vol. 8, no. 3, 1975) 21–24.

Nostra Aetate, 1965	Vatican Guidelines, 1974	Notes for Preaching and Catechesis, 1985
2) — makes no mention of the post-biblical religious tradition of Judaism.	— "The history of Judaism did not end with the destruction of Jerusalem but rather went on to develop a religious tradition" (III, 7). — associates "Jewish and Christian tradition" (IV, 1).	— contains an entire section on "Judaism and Christianity in History" (VI, 25): "The permanence of Israel (while so many ancient peoples have disappeared without a trace) is a historic fact and a sign to be interpreted within God's design . . . accompanied by a continuous spiritual fecundity, in the rabbinical period, in the Middle Ages, and in modern times."
3) — "the spiritual bonds which tie the people of the New Covenant to the off-spring of Abraham" (4, § 1).	— "the spiritual bonds and historical links binding the Church and Judaism" — "these links and relationships" (Intro., § 5).	— "Because of the unique relations that exist between Christianity and Judaism— 'linked together at the very level of their identity' (John Paul II, March 6, 1982)— relations "founded on the design of the God of the Covenant (ibid.), the Jews and Judaism should not occupy an occasional or marginal place in catechesis: their presence there is essential and should be organically integrated" (I, 2).
4) — makes no reference to traditional false stereotyping of the Pharisees or to misunderstandings which can arise from reading the N.T. or in the liturgy.	— mandates an "overriding preoccupation" in liturgy and education to provide adequate background for scriptural readings "which Christians, if not well informed, might misunderstand because of prejudice," and specifies John's Gospel and the treatment of the Pharisees (II, 5).	— Two major sections of the text (III and IV) spell out the issues in detail, e.g.,: Jesus "extolled respect for" the Law and "invited obedience to it" (III, 13). He shared "with the majority of Palestinian Jews of that time," central elements of Pharisaic doctrine (III, 17). ". . . references hostile or less than favorable to the

Nostra Aetate, 1965	*Vatican Guidelines, 1974*	*Notes for Preaching and Catechesis, 1985*
		Jews have their historic context in conflicts between the nascent church and the Jewish community. Certain controversies reflect Christian-Jewish relations long after the time of Jesus" (IV, 21, A).
5) — defines the Jews solely in biblical terms, i.e., in reference to their past: "the Jewish religion," the "chosen people," the "wild olive shoots," "the Jews" (8 times always in the context of the N.T.). Limits itself to "the spiritual patrimony common to Christians and Jews."	— speaks of the Jews of today as well as biblically, and in modern terms "Judaism," "Jewish brothers," "the Jewish people" (twice, and in specifically religious context, being followed immediately by "the Christian people"). Encourages Christians to learn "by what essential traits the Jews define themselves in the light of their own religious tradition" (IV, 1).	— Citing John Paul II, calls the "common patrimony" of the church and Judaism "considerable" calling on catechists and preachers "to assess it carefully in itself and with due awareness of the faith and religious life of the Jewish people as they are professed and practised still today" (I, 3; cf. VI, 25). In this context, mentions the Holocaust and the State of Israel as proper subjects for affirmative Catholic teaching (VI, 25).
6) — makes no reference to the Holocaust of European Jewry.	— refers to the Holocaust as the "historical setting" of *Nostra Aetate* and the present Jewish/Christian dialogue.	— mandates the development of Holocaust curricula in religious education programming: "catechesis should ... help in understanding the meaning for the Jews of the extermination [Shoah] during the years 1939–45, and its consequences" (VI, 25).
7) — no reference to State of Israel.	— no reference to State of Israel.	— speaks of the "religious attachment" between the Jewish covenantal "fidelity to the one God." Affirms "the existence of the biblical tradition" and as an essen-

Nostra Aetate, 1965	*Vatican Guidelines, 1974*	*Notes for Preaching and Catechesis, 1985*
		tial aspect of Jewish covenantal "fidelity to the one God." Affirms "the existence of the State of Israel" on the basis of "the common principles of international law," while warning against a biblical fundamentalist approach to contemporary "political options" in the Middle East (VI, 25).
8) — Crucifixion "cannot be blamed on all Jews then living without distinction nor upon the Jews of today . . . Christ freely underwent his Passion and death because of the sins of all men."	— Repeats *Nostra Aetate*.	— Adds details: Christians more responsible than "those few Jews" because we sin knowingly (IV, 22). ". . . the Pharisees are not mentioned in accounts of the Passion" (III, 19).
9) — Does not try to deal with significance of the Jewish "no" to Christian claims concerning Jesus and the significance of the Christ event.	— Calls on Christians to "strive to understand the difficulties which arise for the Jewish soul—rightly imbued with an extremely high, pure notion of the divine transcendence—when faced with the mystery of the incarnate word" (I).	— Begins to grapple with it as "a fact not merely of history but of theological bearing of which St. Paul tries hard to plumb the meaning" (IV, 21, C and F) and hints at a positive response to "the permanence of Israel" as "a sign to be interpreted within God's design" (VI, 25).
10) — presents the Church as the new people of God (4, § 6).	— avoids supercessionist implications and states instead: "The Old Testament and the Jewish tradition founded on it must not be set against the New Testament in such a way that the former seems to constitute a religion of only justice, fear and legalism with no appeal to the love of God and neighbor (Dt 6:5, Lv 19:18)".	— Jews are to be presented as "the people of God of the Old Covenant, which has never been revoked by God" (I, 3, citing John Paul II at Mainz, Nov. 17, 1980), and "a chosen people" (VI, 25). *Both* Jews and Christians "are driven . . . by the command to love our neighbour" (II, 11).

Nostra Aetate, 1965	*Vatican Guidelines, 1974*	*Notes for Preaching and Catechesis, 1985*
11) — does not deal, as such, with the "promise/fulfillment" theme.	— Distinguishes "fulfillment" of the promises in Christ from "their perfect fulfillment in his glorious return at the end of time" (II).	— "... the people of God of the Old and the New Testament are tending towards a like end in the future: the coming or return of the Messiah—even if they start from different points of view" (II, 9: cf. also II, 1–2 and I, 5).
12) — does not deal with typology.	— does not deal with typology.	— terms typology "perhaps the sign of a problem unresolved." Attempts to frame the question in terms of *both* the Church and Judaism as "awaiting" their "definitive perfecting" and "final consummation" in the End Time (II, 4–9). Allows for other models for relating the Scriptures (II, 2).
13) — no direct reference to joint witness to the world, though the possibility is implicit in the affirmation that God "does not repent of the gifts He makes or of the calls He issues."	— "Jewish and Christian tradition, founded on the Word of God ... will work willingly together, seeking social justice and peace on every level" (IV).	— "... hanging on the same word, we have to witness to one same memory and one common hope in Him ... We must also accept our responsibility to prepare the world for the coming of the Messiah by working together for social justice ... To this we are driven ... by a common hope for the Kingdom of God" (II, 11).
14) — no explicit acknowledgment of the validity of Jewish witness, to the Church or to the world, *post*	— still implicit, e.g. in IV.	— "A numerous Diaspora ... allowed Israel to carry to the whole world a witness—often heroic—of its

Nostra Aetate, 1965   *Vatican Guidelines, 1974*   *Notes for Preaching and
                                                                          Catechesis, 1985*

Christum. Implicit in pres-   fidelity to the one God and
ent-tense translation of   to exalt Him in the presence
phrase from St. Paul: of all the living" (VI, 25).
"Theirs *are* the sonship and   Affirms that Christian cate-
the glory and the Covenant   chesis cannot adequately
and the law and the worship   convey the Christian mes-
and the promises" (Rm   sage without taking into ac-
9:4–5). Many Christian   count past and present Jew-
translations of the New Tes-   ish tradition (I, 2–3; II, 11;
tament (e.g. the *New Ameri-*   III, 12, 17–18, 20; VI, 25).
can Bible) had tended to
translate this key phrase in
the past tense: ". . . theirs
were . . . ."

II.
VATICAN DOCUMENTS ON CATHOLIC-JEWISH RELATIONS

1. Declaration on the Relationship of the Church to Non-Christian Religions [*Nostra Aetate* (no. 4) (October 28, 1965)]

Ecumenical Council Vatican II

As this sacred Synod searches into the mystery of the church, it recalls the spiritual bond linking the people of the new covenant with Abraham's stock.

For the church of Christ acknowledges that, according to the mystery of God's saving design, the beginnings of her faith and her election are already found among the patriarchs, Moses, and the prophets. She professes that all who believe in Christ, Abraham's sons according to faith (cf. Ga 3:7), are included in the same patriarch's call, and likewise that the salvation of the church was mystically foreshadowed by the chosen people's exodus from the land of bondage.

The church, therefore, cannot forget that she received the revelation of the Old Testament through the people with whom God in his inexpressible mercy deigned to establish the ancient covenant. Nor can she forget that she draws sustenance from the root of that good olive tree onto which have been grafted the wild olive branches of the Gentiles (cf. Rm 11:17–24). Indeed, the church believes that by His cross Christ, our Peace, reconciled Jew and Gentile, making them both one in himself (cf. Ep 2:14–16).

Also, the church ever keeps in mind the words of the apostle about his kinsmen, "who have the adoption as sons, and the glory and the covenant and the legislation and the worship and the promise; who have the fathers, and from whom is Christ according to the flesh" (Rm 9:4–5), the son of the Virgin Mary. The church recalls too that from the Jewish people sprang the apostles, her foundation stones and pillars, as well as most of the early disciples who proclaimed Christ to the world.

As holy scripture testifies, Jerusalem did not recognize the time of her visitation (cf. Lk 19:44), nor did the Jews in large number accept the gospel; indeed, not a few opposed the spreading of it (cf. Rm 11:28). Nevertheless, according to the apostle, the Jews still remain most dear to God because of their fathers, for He does not repent of the gifts He makes nor of the calls He issues (cf. Rm 11:28-29). In company with the prophets and the same apostle, the church awaits that day, known to God alone, on which all peoples will address the Lord in a single voice and "serve Him with one accord" (Soph 3:9; cf. Is 66:23; Ps 65:4; Rm 11:11-32).

Since the spiritual patrimony common to Christians and Jews is thus so great, this sacred Synod wishes to foster and recommend that mutual understanding and respect which is the fruit above all of biblical and theological studies, and of brotherly dialogues.

True, authorities of the Jews and those who followed their lead pressed for the death of Christ (cf. Jn 19:6); still, what happened in His passion cannot be blamed upon all the Jews then living, without distinction, nor upon the Jews of today. Although the church is the new people of God, the Jews should not be presented as repudiated or cursed by God, as if such views followed from the holy scriptures. All should take pains, then, lest in catechetical instruction and in the preaching of God's word they teach anything out of harmony with the truth of the gospel and the spirit of Christ.

The church repudiates all persecutions against any man. Moreover, mindful of her common patrimony with the Jews, and motivated by the gospel's spiritual love and by no political considerations, she deplores the hatred, persecutions, and displays of anti-Semitism directed against the Jews at any time and from any source.

Besides, as the church has always held and continues to hold, Christ in His boundless love freely underwent His passion and death because of the sins of all men, so that all might attain salvation. It is, therefore, the duty of the church's preaching to proclaim the cross of Christ as the sign of God's all-embracing love and as the fountain from which every grace flows.

2. Guidelines and Suggestions for Implementing the Conciliar Declaration *Nostra Aetate* (no. 4) [December 1, 1974]

Vatican Commission for Religious Relations with the Jews

Introductory Note

The document is published over the signature of Cardinal Willebrands, in his capacity as President of the new Commission for the Catholic Church's religious relations with the Jews, instituted by Paul VI on 22 October 1974. It comes out a short time after the ninth anniversary of the promulgation of *Nostra Aetate,* the Second Vatican Council's Declaration on the Church's relations with non-Christian religions.

The "Guidelines and Suggestions," which refer to no. 4 of the Declaration, are notable for their almost exclusively practical nature and for their sobriety.

This deliberately practical nature of the text is justified by the fact that it concerns a pragmatic document.

It does not propose a Christian theology of Judaism. Such a theology certainly has an interest for specialist research and reflection, but it still needs considerable study. The new Commission for Religious Relations with the Jews should be able to play a part in the gradual fruition of this endeavour.

The *first part* of the Document recalls the principal teachings of the council on the condemnation of anti-Semitism and of all discrimination, and the obligation of reciprocal understanding and of renewed mutual esteem. It also hopes for a better knowledge on the part of Christians of the essence of the religious tradition of Judaism and of the manner in which Jews identify themselves.

The text then proposes a series of concrete suggestions.

The section dedicated to *dialogue* calls for fraternal dialogue and the establishment of deep doctrinal research. Prayer in common is also proposed as a means of encounter.

With regard to the *liturgy,* mention is made of the links between the Christian liturgy and the Jewish liturgy and of the caution which is needed in dealing with commentaries on biblical texts, and with liturgical explanations and translations.

The part concerning *teaching* and *education* allows the relations between the two touched upon and stress is laid on the note of expectation which characterizes both the Jewish and the Christian religion. Specialists are invited to conduct serious research and the establishment of chairs of Hebrew studies is encouraged where it is possible, as well as collaboration with Jewish scholars.

The final section deals with the possibilities of *common social action* in the context of a search for social justice and for peace.

The *conclusion* touches on, among other things, the ecumenical aspect of the problem of relations with Judaism, the initiatives of local churches in this area, and the essential lines of the mission of the new Commission instituted by the Holy See.

The great sobriety of the text is noted also in the concrete suggestions which it puts forward. But it would certainly be wrong to interpret such sobriety as being indicative of a limiting programme of activities. The document does propose limited suggestions for some key sectors, but it is a document meant for the universal Church, and as such it cannot take account of all the individual situations. The suggestions put forward are intended to give ideas to those who were asking themselves how to start on a local level that dialogue which the text invites them to begin and to develop. These suggestions are mentioned because of their value as examples. They are made because it seems that they could find ample application and that their proposal at the same time constitutes an apt programme for aiding local churches to organize their own activities, in order to harmonize with the general movement of the universal Church in dialogue with Judaism.

The Document can be considered from a certain point of view as the Commission's first step for the realization of religious relations with Judaism. It will devolve on the new Commission to prepare and put forward, when necessary, the further developments which may seem necessary in order that the initiative of the Second Vatican Council in this important area may continue to bear fruit on a local and on a worldwide level, for the benefit of peace of heart and harmony of spirit of all who work under the protection of the one Almighty God.

The Document, which gives the invitation to an effort of mutual understanding and collaboration, coincides with the opening of the Holy Year, which is consecrated to the theme of reconciliation. It is impossible not to perceive in such a coincidence an invitation to study and to apply in concrete terms throughout the whole world the suggestions which the Document proposes. Likewise one cannot fail to hope that our Jewish brothers too may find in it useful indications for their participation in a commitment which is common.

PREAMBLE

The Declaration *Nostra Aetate,* issued by the Second Vatican Council on 28 October 1965, "on the relationship of the Church to non-Christian religions" (no. 4), marks an important milestone in the history of Jewish-Christian relations.

Moreover, the step taken by the council finds its historical setting in circumstances deeply affected by the memory of the persecution and massacre of Jews which took place in Europe just before and during the Second World War.

Although Christianity sprang from Judaism, taking from it certain essential elements of its faith and divine cult, the gap dividing them was deepened more and more, to such an extent that Christian and Jew hardly knew each other.

After two thousand years, too often marked by mutual ignorance and frequent confrontation, the Declaration *Nostra Aetate* provides an opportunity to open or to continue a dialogue with a view to better mutual understanding. Over the past nine years, many steps in this direction have been taken in various countries. As a result, it is easier to distinguish the conditions under which a new relationship between Jews and Christians may be worked out and developed. This seems the right moment to propose, following the guidelines of the council, some concrete suggestions born of experience, hoping that they will help to bring into actual existence in the life of the Church the intentions expressed in the conciliar document.

While referring the reader back to this document, we may simply restate here that the spiritual bonds and historical links binding the

Church to Judaism condemn (as opposed to the very spirit of Christianity) all forms of anti-Semitism and discrimination, which in any case the dignity of the human person alone would suffice to condemn. Further still, these links and relationships render obligatory a better mutual understanding and renewed mutual esteem. On the practical level in particular, Christians must therefore strive to acquire a better knowledge of the basic components of the religious tradition of Judaism; they must strive to learn by what essential traits the Jews define themselves in the light of their own religious experience.

With due respect for such matters of principle, we simply propose some first practical applications in different essential areas of the Church's life, with a view to launching or developing sound relations between Catholics and their Jewish brothers.

I. Dialogue

To tell the truth, such relations as there have been between Jew and Christian have scarcely ever risen above the level of monologue. From now on, real dialogue must be established.

Dialogue presupposes that each side wishes to know the other, and wishes to increase and deepen its knowledge of the other. It constitutes a particularly suitable means of favoring a better mutual knowledge and, especially in the case of dialogue between Jews and Christians, of probing the riches of one's own tradition. Dialogue demands respect for the other as he is; above all respect for his faith and his religious convictions.

In virtue of her divine mission, and her very nature, the Church must preach Jesus Christ to the world (*Ad Gentes*, 2). Lest the witness of Catholics to Jesus Christ should give offense to Jews, they must take care to live and spread their Christian faith while maintaining the strictest respect for religious liberty in line with the teaching of the Second Vatican Council (Declaration *Dignitatis Humanae*). They will likewise strive to understand the difficulties which arise for the Jewish soul—rightly imbued with an extremely high, pure notion of the divine transcendence —when faced with the mystery of the incarnate Word.

While it is true that a widespread air of suspicion, inspired by an unfortunate past, is still dominant in this particular area, Christians, for their part, will be able to see to what extent the responsibility is theirs and deduce practical conclusions for the future.

In addition to friendly talks, competent people will be encouraged to meet and to study together the many problems deriving from the fundamental convictions of Judaism and of Christianity. In order not to hurt (even involuntarily) those taking part, it will be vital to guarantee, not only tact, but a great openness of spirit and diffidence with respect to one's own prejudices.

In whatever circumstances as shall prove possible and mutually acceptable, one might encourage a common meeting in the presence of God, in prayer and silent meditation, a highly efficacious way of finding that humility, that openness of heart and mind, necessary prerequisites for a deep knowledge of oneself and of others. In particular, that will be done in connection with great causes such as the struggle for peace and justice.

II. Liturgy

The existing links between the Christian liturgy and the Jewish liturgy will be borne in mind. The idea of a living community in the service of God, and in the service of men for the love of God, such as it is realized in the liturgy, is just as characteristic of the Jewish liturgy as it is of the Christian one. To improve Jewish-Christian relations, it is important to take cognizance of those common elements of the liturgical life (formulas, feasts, rites, etc.) in which the Bible holds an essential place.

An effort will be made to acquire a better understanding of whatever in the Old Testament retains its own perpetual value (cf. *Dei Verbum,* 14–15), since that has not been cancelled by the later interpretation of the New Testament. Rather, the New Testament brings out the full meaning of the Old, while both Old and New illumine and explain each other (cf. *ibid.,* 16). This is all the more important since liturgical reform is now bringing the text of the Old Testament ever more frequently to the attention of Christians.

When commenting on biblical texts, emphasis will be laid on the continuity of our faith with that of the earlier Covenant, in the perspective of the promises, without minimizing those elements of Christianity which are original. We believe that those promises were fulfilled with the first coming of Christ. But it is none the less true that we still await their perfect fulfillment in his glorious return at the end of time.

With respect to liturgical readings, care will be taken to see that homilies based on them will not distort their meaning, especially when it is a question of passages which seem to show the Jewish people as such in an unfavourable light. Efforts will be made so to instruct the Christian people that they will understand the true interpretation of all the texts and their meaning for the contemporary believer.

Commissions entrusted with the task of liturgical translation will pay particular attention to the way in which they express those phrases and passages which Christians, if not well informed, might misunderstand because of prejudice. Obviously, one cannot alter the text of the Bible. The point is that, with a version destined for liturgical use, there should be an overriding preoccupation to bring out explicitly the meaning of a text,[1] while taking scriptural studies into account.

The preceding remarks also apply to introductions to biblical readings, to the Prayer of the Faithful, and to commentaries printed in missals used by the laity.

III. Teaching and Education

Although there is still a great deal of work to be done, a better understanding of Judaism itself and its relationship to Christianity has been achieved in recent years thanks to the teaching of the church, the study and research of scholars, as also to the beginning of dialogue.

In this respect, the following facts deserve to be recalled:
— It is the same God, "inspirer and author of the books of both Testaments" (*Dei Verbum*, 16), who speaks both in the old and new Covenants.
— Judaism in the time of Christ and the Apostles was a complex reality, embracing many different trends, many spiritual, religious, social and cultural values.
— The Old Testament and the Jewish tradition founded upon it must not be set against the New Testament in such a way that the former seems to constitute a religion of only justice, fear and legalism, with no appeal to the love of God and neighbor (cf. Dt 6:5; Lv 19:18; Mt 22:34–40).
— Jesus was born of the Jewish people, as were his Apostles and a large number of his first disciples. When he revealed himself as

---

1. Thus the formula "the Jews," in St. John, sometimes according to the context means "the leaders of the Jews," or "the adversaries of Jesus," terms which express better the thought of the evangelist and avoid appearing to arraign the Jewish people as such. Another example is the use of the words "Pharisee" and "Pharisaism" which have taken on a largely pejorative meaning.

the Messiah and Son of God (cf. Mt 16:16), the bearer of the new gospel message, he did so as the fulfilment and perfection of the earlier Revelation. And, although his teaching had a profoundly new character, Christ, nevertheless, in many instances, took his stand on the teaching of the Old Testament. The New Testament is profoundly marked by its relation to the Old. As the Second Vatican Council declared: "God, the inspirer and author of the books of both Testaments, wisely arranged that the New Testament be hidden in the Old and the Old be made manifest in the New" (*Dei Verbum,* 16). Jesus also used teaching methods similar to those employed by the rabbis of his time.

— With regard to the trial and death of Jesus, the Council recalled that "what happened in his passion cannot be blamed upon all the Jews then living, without distinction, nor upon the Jews of today" (*Nostra Aetate,* 4).

— The history of Judaism did not end with the destruction of Jerusalem, but rather went on to develop a religious tradition. And, although we believe that the importance and meaning of that tradition were deeply affected by the coming of Christ, it is still nonetheless rich in religious values.

— With the prophets and the apostle Paul, "the church awaits the day, known to God alone, on which all peoples will address the Lord in a single voice and 'serve Him with one accord' (Soph 3:9)" (*Nostra Aetate,* 4).

Information concerning these questions is important at all levels of Christian instruction and education. Among sources of information, special attention should be paid to the following:

— catechism and religious textbooks;

— history books;

— the mass-media (press, radio, cinema, television).

The effective use of these means presupposes the thorough formation of instructors and educators in training schools, seminaries and universities.

Research into the problems bearing on Judaism and Jewish-Christian relations will be encouraged among specialists, particularly in the fields of exegesis, theology, history and sociology. Higher institutions of Catholic research, in association if possible with other similar Christian institutions and experts, are invited to contribute to the solution of such problems. Wherever possible, chairs of Jewish studies will be created, and collaboration with Jewish scholars encouraged.

IV. Joint Social Action

Jewish and Christian tradition, founded on the Word of God, is aware of the value of the human person, the image of God. Love of the same God must show itself in effective action for the good of mankind. In the spirit of the prophets, Jews and Christians will work willingly together, seeking social justice and peace at every level—local, national and international.

At the same time, such collaboration can do much to foster mutual understanding and esteem.

Conclusion

The Second Vatican Council has pointed out the path to follow in promoting deep fellowship between Jews and Christians. But there is still a long road ahead.

The problem of Jewish-Christian relations concerns the Church as such, since it is when "pondering her own mystery" that she encounters the mystery of Israel. Therefore, even in areas where no Jewish communities exist, this remains an important problem. There is also an ecumenical aspect to the question: the very return of Christians to the sources and origins of their faith, grafted on to the earlier Covenant, helps the search for unity in Christ, the cornerstone.

In this field, the bishops will know what best to do on the pastoral level, within the general disciplinary framework of the Church and in line with the common teaching of her magisterium. For example, they will create some suitable commissions or secretariats on a national or regional level, or appoint some competent person to promote the implementation of the conciliar directives and the suggestions made above.

On 22 October 1974, the Holy Father instituted for the universal Church this Commission for Religious Relations with the Jews, joined to the Secretariat for Promoting Christian Unity. This special Commission, created to encourage and foster religious relations between Jews and Catholics—and to do so eventually in collaboration with other Christians—will be, within the limits of its competence, at the service of all interested organizations, providing information for them, and helping them to pursue their task in conformity with the instructions of the Holy See.

The Commission wishes to develop this collaboration in order to implement, correctly and effectively, the express intentions of the council.

Given at Rome, 1 December 1974.

✠JOHANNES CARD. WILLEBRANDS
President of the Commission

PIERRE-MARIE DE CONTENSON, OP
Secretary of the Commission

3. Notes on the Correct Way to Present the Jews and Judaism in Preaching and Catechesis in the Roman Catholic Church [June 24, 1985]

Vatican Commission for Religious Relations with the Jews

Preliminary Considerations

On March 6th, 1982, Pope John Paul II told delegates of episcopal conferences and other experts, meeting in Rome to study relations between the church and Judaism:

> ". . . you yourselves were concerned, during your sessions, with Catholic teaching and catechesis regarding Jews and Judaism. . . . We should aim, in this field, that Catholic teaching at its different levels, in catechesis to children and young people, presents Jews and Judaism, not only in an honest and objective manner, free from prejudices and without any offences, but also with full awareness of the heritage common" to Jews and Christians.

In this passage, so charged with meaning, the Holy Father plainly drew inspiration from the Council Declaration *Nostra Aetate,* 4, which says:

> "All should take pains, then, lest in catechetical instruction and in the preaching of God's Word they teach anything out of harmony with the truth of the gospel and the spirit of Christ";

as also from these words:

> "Since the spiritual patrimony common to Christians and Jews is thus
> so great, this sacred Synod wishes to foster and recommend mutual
> understanding and respect. . . ."

In the same way, the *Guidelines and Suggestions for implementing
the Conciliar declaration Nostra Aetate (no. 4)* ends its chapter III, entitled "Teaching and education," which lists a number of practical things
to be done, with this recommendation:

> "Information concerning these questions is important at all levels of
> Christian instruction and education. Among sources of information,
> special attention should be paid to the following:
> — catechisms and religious textbooks;
> — history books;
> — the mass media (press, radio, cinema, television).
> The effective use of these means presupposes the thorough for-
> mation of instructors and educators in training schools, seminaries and
> universities" (*AAS* 77 [1975] 73).

The paragraphs which follow are intended to serve this purpose.

I. RELIGIOUS TEACHING AND JUDAISM

1. In *Nostra Aetate,* 4, the Council speaks of the "spiritual bonds
linking" Jews and Christians and of the "great spiritual patrimony"
common to both and it further asserts that "the Church of Christ acknowledges that, according to the mystery of God's saving design, the
beginning of her faith and her election are already found among the
patriarchs, Moses and the prophets."

2. Because of the unique relations that exist between Christianity
and Judaism—"linked together at the very level of their identity" (John
Paul II, 6th March, 1982)—relations "founded on the design of the God
of the Covenant" (ibid.), the Jews and Judaism should not occupy an
occasional and marginal place in catechesis: their presence there is essential and should be organically integrated.

3. This concern for Judaism in Catholic teaching has not merely a
historical or archeological foundation. As the Holy Father said in the
speech already quoted, after he had again mentioned the "common patrimony" of the Church and Judaism as "considerable": "To assess it

carefully in itself and with due awareness of the faith and religious life of the Jewish people *as they are professed and practiced still today,* can greatly help us to understand better certain aspects of the life of the Church" (italics added). It is a question then of *pastoral* concern for a still living reality closely related to the Church. The Holy Father has stated this permanent reality of the Jewish people in a remarkable theological formula, in his allocution to the Jewish community of West Germany at Mainz, on November 17th, 1980: ". . . the people of God of the Old Covenant, which has never been revoked. . . ."

4. Here we should recall the passage in which the *Guidelines and Suggestions,* I, tried to define the fundamental condition of dialogue: "respect for the other as he is," knowledge of the "basic components of the religious tradition of Judaism" and again learning "by what essential traits the Jews define themselves in the light of their own religious experience" (*Introd.*).

5. The singular character and the difficulty of Christian teaching about Jews and Judaism lies in this, that it needs to balance a number of pairs of ideas which express the relation between the two economies of the Old and New Testaments:

Promise and Fulfilment
Continuity and Newness
Singularity and Universality
Uniqueness and Exemplary Nature.

This means that the theologian and the catechist who deals with the subject needs to show in his practice of teaching that:
— promise and fulfilment throw light on each other;
— newness lies in a metamorphosis of what was there before;
— the singularity of the people of the Old Testament is not exclusive and is open, in the divine vision, to a universal extension;
— the uniqueness of the Jewish people is meant to have the force of an example.

6. Finally, "work that is of poor quality and lacking in precision would be extremely detrimental" to Judaeo-Christian dialogue (John Paul II, speech of March 6th, 1982). But it would be above all detrimental—since we are talking of teaching and education—to Christian identity (ibid.).

7. "In virtue of her divine mission, the Church" which is to be "the all-embracing means of salvation" in which alone "the fullness of the

means of salvation can be obtained" (*Unitatis Redintegratio,* 3), "must of her nature proclaim Jesus Christ to the world" (cf. *Guidelines and Suggestions,* I). Indeed we believe that it is through Him that we go to the Father (cf. Jn 14:6) "and this is eternal life, that they know Thee the only true God and Jesus Christ whom Thou hast sent" (Jn 17:3).

Jesus affirms (ibid. 10:16) that "there shall be one flock and one shepherd". Church and Judaism cannot then be seen as two parallel ways of salvation and the Church must witness to Christ as the Redeemer for all, "while maintaining the strictest respect for religious liberty in line with the teaching of the Second Vatican Council (Declaration *Dignitatis Humanae*" (*Guidelines and Suggestions,* I).

8. The urgency and importance of precise, objective and rigorously accurate teaching on Judaism for our faithful follows too from the danger of anti-Semitism which is always ready to reappear under different guises. The question is not merely to uproot from among the faithful the remains of anti-Semitism still to be found here and there, but much rather to arouse in them, through educational work, an exact knowledge of the wholly unique "bond" (*Nostra Aetate,* 4) which joins us as a Church to the Jews and to Judaism. In this way, they would learn to appreciate and love the latter, who have been chosen by God to prepare the coming of Christ and have preserved everything that was progressively revealed and given in the course of that preparation, notwithstanding their difficulty in recognising in Him their Messiah.

II. RELATIONS BETWEEN THE OLD[1] AND NEW TESTAMENT

1. Our aim should be to show the unity of Biblical Revelation (O.T. and N.T.) and of the divine plan, before speaking of each historical event, so as to stress that particular events have meaning when seen in history as a whole—from creation to fulfilment. This history concerns the whole human race and especially believers. Thus the definitive meaning of the election of Israel does not become clear except in the light of the complete fulfilment (Rm 9–11) and election in Jesus Christ is still better understood with reference to the announcement and the promise (cf. Heb 4:1–11).

---

1. We continue to use the expression *Old Testament* because it is traditional (cf. already 2 Co 3:14) but also because "Old" does not mean "out of date" or "outworn." In any case, it is the *permanent* value of the O.T. as a source of Christian Revelation that is emphasised here (cf. *Dei Verbum,* 3).

2. We are dealing with singular happenings which concern a singular nation but are destined, in the sight of God who reveals His purpose, to take on universal and exemplary significance.

The aim is moreover to present the events of the Old Testament not as concerning only the Jews but also as touching us personally. Abraham is truly the father of our faith (cf. Rm 4:11–12; Roman Canon: *patriarchae nostri Abrahae*). And it is said (1 Co 10:1): "*Our* fathers were all under the cloud, and all passed through the sea." The patriarchs, prophets and other personalities of the Old Testament have been venerated and always will be venerated as saints in the liturgical tradition of the Oriental Church as also of the Latin Church.

3. From the unity of the divine plan derives the problem of the relation between the Old and New Testaments. The Church already from apostolic times (cf. 1 Co 10:11; Heb 10:1) and then constantly in tradition resolved this problem by means of typology, which emphasises the primordial value that the Old Testament must have in the Christian view. Typology, however, makes many people uneasy and is perhaps the sign of a problem unresolved.

4. Hence, in using typology, the teaching and practice which we have received from the Liturgy and from the Fathers of the Church, we should be careful to avoid any transition from the Old to the New Testament which might seem merely a rupture. The Church, in the spontaneity of the Spirit which animates her, has vigorously condemned the attitude of Marcion[2] and always opposed his dualism.

5. It should also be emphasised that typological interpretation consists in reading the Old Testament as preparation and, in certain aspects, outline and foreshadowing of the New (cf., e.g., Heb 5:5–10, etc.). Christ is henceforth the key and point of reference to the Scriptures: "the rock *was* Christ" (1 Co 10:4).

6. It is true then, and should be stressed, that the Church and Christians read the Old Testament in the light of the event of the dead and risen Christ and that on these grounds there is a Christian reading of the Old Testament which does not necessarily coincide with the Jewish reading. Thus Christian identity and Jewish identity should be carefully distinguished in their respective reading of the Bible. But this detracts noth-

---

2. A man of gnostic tendency who in the second century rejected the Old Testament and part of the New as the work of an evil god, a demiurge. The Church reacted strongly against this heresy (cf. Irenaeus).

ing from the value of the Old Testament in the Church and does nothing to hinder Christians from profiting discerningly from the traditions of Jewish reading.

7. Typological reading only manifests the unfathomable riches of the Old Testament, its inexhaustible content and the mystery of which it is full, and should not lead us to forget that it retains its own value as Revelation that the New Testament often does no more than resume (cf. Mk 12:29-31). Moreover, the New Testament itself demands to be read in the light of the Old. Primitive Christian catechesis constantly had recourse to this (cf., e.g., 1 Co 5:6-8; 10:1-11).

8. Typology further signifies reaching towards the accomplishment of the divine plan, when "God will be all in all" (1 Cor 15:28). This holds true also for the Church which, realised already in Christ, yet awaits its definitive perfecting as the Body of Christ. The fact that the Body of Christ is still tending towards its full stature (cf. Ep 4:12-19) takes nothing from the value of being a Christian. So also the calling of the patriarchs and the Exodus from Egypt do not lose their importance and value in God's design from being at the same time intermediate stages (cf., e.g., *Nostra Aetate,* 4).

9. The Exodus, for example, represents an experience of salvation and liberation that is not complete in itself, but has in it, over and above its own meaning, the capacity to be developed further. Salvation and liberation are already accomplished in Christ and gradually realised by the sacraments in the Church. This makes way for the fulfilment of God's design, which awaits its final consummation with the return of Jesus as Messiah, for which we pray each day. The Kingdom, for the coming of which we also pray each day, will be finally established. With salvation and liberation the elect and the whole of Creation will be transformed in Christ (Rm 8:19-23).

10. Furthermore, in underlining the eschatological dimension of Christianity we shall reach a greater awareness that the people of God of the Old and the New Testament are tending towards a like end in the future: the coming or return of the Messiah—even if they start from two different points of view. It is more clearly understood that the person of the Messiah is not only a point of division for the people of God but also a point of convergence (cf. *Sussidi per l'ecumenismo* of the diocese of Rome, n. 140). Thus it can be said that Jews and Christians meet in a comparable hope, founded on the same promise made to Abraham (cf. Gn 12:1-3; Heb 6:13-18).

11. Attentive to the same God who has spoken, hanging on the

same word, we have to witness to one same memory and one common hope in Him who is the master of history. We must also accept our responsibility to prepare the world for the coming of the Messiah by working together for social justice, respect for the rights of persons and nations and for social and international reconciliation. To this we are driven, Jews and Christians, by the command to love our neighbor, by a common hope for the Kingdom of God and by the great heritage of the Prophets. Transmitted soon enough by catechesis, such a conception would teach young Christians in a practical way to cooperate with Jews, going beyond simple dialogue (cf. *Guidelines,* IV).

III. JEWISH ROOTS OF CHRISTIANITY

12. Jesus was and always remained a Jew, his ministry was deliberately limited "to the lost sheep of the house of Israel" (Mt 15:24). Jesus is fully a man of his time, and of his environment—the Jewish Palestinian one of the first century, the anxieties and hopes of which he shared. This cannot but underline both the reality of the Incarnation and the very meaning of the history of salvation, as it has been revealed in the Bible (cf. Rm 1:3–4; Ga 4:4–5).

13. Jesus' relations with biblical law and its more or less traditional interpretations are undoubtedly complex and he showed great liberty towards it (cf. the "antitheses" of the Sermon on the Mount: Mt 5:21–48, bearing in mind the exegetical difficulties; his attitude to rigorous observance of the Sabbath: Mk 3:1–6, etc.).

But there is no doubt that he wished to submit himself to the law (cf. Ga 4:4), that he was circumcised and presented in the Temple like any Jew of his time (cf. Lk 2:21, 22–24), that he was trained in the law's observance. He extolled respect for it (cf. Mt 5:17–20) and invited obedience to it (cf. Mt 8:4). The rhythm of his life was marked by observance of pilgrimages on great feasts, even from his infancy (cf. Lk 2:41–50; Jn 2:13; 7–10, etc.). The importance of the cycle of the Jewish feasts has been frequently underlined in the Gospel of John (cf. 2:13; 5:1; 7:2.10.37; 10:22; 12:1; 13:1; 18:28; 19:42, etc.).

14. It should be noted also that Jesus often taught in the Synagogues (cf. Mt 4:23; 9:35; Lk 4:15–18; Jn 18:20, etc.) and in the Temple (cf. Jn 18:20, etc.), which he frequented as did the disciples even after the Resurrection (cf., e.g., Ac 2:46; 3:1; 21:26, etc.). He wished to put in the context of synagogue worship the proclamation of his Messiahship (cf. Lk 4:16–21). But above all he wished to achieve the supreme act of the gift of

himself in the setting of the domestic liturgy of the Passover, or at least of the paschal festivity (cf. Mk 14:1.12 and parallels; Jn 18:28). This also allows of a better understanding of the "memorial" character of the Eucharist.

15. Thus the Son of God is incarnate in a people and a human family (cf. Ga 4:4; Rm 9:5). This takes away nothing, quite the contrary, from the fact that he was born for all men (Jewish shepherds and pagan wise men are found at his crib: Lk 2:8–20; Mt 2:1–12) and died for all men (at the foot of the cross there are Jews, among them Mary and John: Jn 19:25–27, and pagans like the centurion: Mk 15:39 and parallels). Thus he made two peoples one in his flesh (cf. Ep 2:14–17). This explains why with the *Ecclesia ex gentibus* we have, in Palestine and elsewhere, an *Ecclesia ex circumcisione,* of which *Eusebius* for example speaks (*H.E.,* IV, 5).

16. His relations with the Pharisees were not always or wholly polemical. Of this there are many proofs:
— It is Pharisees who warn Jesus of the risks he is running (Lk 13:31);
— Some Pharisees are praised—e.g., "the scribe" of Mk 12:34;
— Jesus eats with Pharisees (Lk 7:36; 14:1).

17. Jesus shares, with the majority of Palestinian Jews of that time, some pharisaic doctrines: the resurrection of the body; forms of piety, like alms-giving, prayer, fasting (cf. Mt 6:1–18) and the liturgical practice of addressing God as Father; the priority of the commandment to love God and our neighbor (cf. Mk 12:28–34). This is so also with Paul (cf. Ac 23:8), who always considered his membership of the Pharisees as a title of honor (cf. ibid., 23:6; 26:5; Ph 3:5).

18. Paul also, like Jesus himself, used methods of reading and interpreting Scripture and of teaching his disciples which were common to the Pharisees of their time. This applies to the use of parables in Jesus' ministry, as also to the method of Jesus and Paul of supporting a conclusion with a quotation from Scripture.

19. It is noteworthy too that the Pharisees are not mentioned in accounts of the Passion. Gamaliel (Ac 5:34–39) defends the apostles in a meeting of the Sanhedrin. An exclusively negative picture of the Pharisees is likely to be inaccurate and unjust (cf. *Guidelines,* Note 1; cf. *AAS,* p. 76). If in the Gospel and elsewhere in the New Testament there are all sorts of unfavorable references to the Pharisees, they should be seen against the background of a complex and diversified movement. Criticisms of various types of Pharisees are moreover not lacking in rabbinical

sources (cf. the *Babylonian Talmud,* the *Sotah* treatise 22b, etc.). "Phariseeism" in the pejorative sense can be rife in any religion. It may also be stressed that, if Jesus shows himself severe towards the Pharisees, it is because he is closer to them than to other contemporary Jewish groups (cf. *supra* no. 17).

20. All this should help us to understand better what St Paul says (Rm 11:16 ff) about the "root" and the "branches." The Church and Christianity, for all their novelty, find their origin in the Jewish milieu of the first century of our era, and more deeply still in the "design of God" (*Nostra Aetate,* 4), realised in the Patriarchs, Moses and the Prophets (ibid.), down to its consummation in Christ Jesus.

IV. THE JEWS IN THE NEW TESTAMENT

21. The *Guidelines* already say (note 1) that "the formula 'the Jews' sometimes, according to the context, means 'the leaders of the Jews' or 'the adversaries of Jesus,' terms which express better the thought of the evangelist and avoid appearing to arraign the Jewish people as such."

An objective presentation of the role of the Jewish people in the New Testament should take account of these various facts:

A) The Gospels are the outcome of long and complicated editorial work. The dogmatic constitution *Dei Verbum,* following the Pontifical Biblical Commission's Instruction *Sancta Mater Ecclesia,* distinguished three stages: "The sacred authors wrote the four Gospels, selecting some things from the many which had been handed on by word of mouth or in writing, reducing some of them to a synthesis, explicating some things in view of the situation of their Churches, and preserving the form of proclamation, but always in such fashion that they told us the honest truth about Jesus" (no. 19).

Hence it cannot be ruled out that some references hostile or less than favorable to the Jews have their historical context in conflicts between the nascent Church and the Jewish community. Certain controversies reflect Christian-Jewish relations long after the time of Jesus.

To establish this is of capital importance if we wish to bring out the meaning of certain Gospel texts for the Christians of today.

All this should be taken into account when preparing catechesis and homilies for the last weeks of Lent and Holy Week (cf. already *Guidelines* II, and now also *Sussidi per l'ecumenismo nella diocesi di Roma,* 1982, 144b).

B) It is clear on the other hand that there were conflicts between

Jesus and certain categories of Jews of his time, among them Pharisees, from the beginning of his ministry (cf. Mk 2:1–11.24; 3:6, etc.).

C) There is moreover the sad fact that the majority of the Jewish people and its authorities did not believe in Jesus—a fact not merely of history but of theological bearing, of which St. Paul tries hard to plumb the meaning (Rm chap. 9–11).

D) This fact, accentuated as the Christian mission developed, especially among the pagans, led inevitably to a rupture between Judaism and the young Church, now irreducibly separated and divergent in faith, and this stage of affairs is reflected in the texts of the New Testament and particularly in the Gospels. There is no question of playing down or glossing over this rupture; that could only prejudice the identity of either side. Nevertheless it certainly does not cancel the spiritual "bond" of which the Council speaks (*Nostra Aetate,* 4) and which we propose to dwell on here.

E) Reflecting on this in the light of Scripture, notably of the chapters cited from the epistle to the Romans, Christians should never forget that the faith is a free gift of God (cf. Rm 9:12) and that we should never judge the consciences of others. St. Paul's exhortation "do not boast" in your attitude to "the root" (Rm 11:18) has its full point here.

F) There is no putting the Jews who knew Jesus and did not believe in him, or those who opposed the preaching of the apostles, on the same plane with Jews who came after or those of today. If the responsibility of the former remains a mystery hidden with God (cf. Rm 11:25), the latter are in an entirely different situation. Vatican II in the declaration on *Religious Liberty* teaches that "all men are to be immune from coercion . . . in such wise that in matters religious no one is to be forced to act in a manner contrary to his own beliefs. Nor . . . restrained from acting in accordance with his own beliefs" (no. 2). This is one of the bases—proclaimed by the Council—on which Judaeo-Christian dialogue rests.

22. The delicate question of responsibility for the death of Christ must be looked at from the standpoint of the conciliar declaration *Nostra Aetate,* 4 and of *Guidelines and Suggestions* (§ III): "What happened in (Christ's) passion cannot be blamed upon all the Jews then living without distinction nor upon the Jews of today," especially since "authorities of the Jews and those who followed their lead pressed for the death of Christ." Again, further on: "Christ in his boundless love freely underwent his passion and death because of the sins of all men, so that all might attain salvation" (*Nostra Aetate,* 4). The *Catechism* of the Council of Trent teaches that Christian sinners are more to blame for the death of

Christ than those few Jews who brought it about—they indeed "knew not what they did" (cf. Lk 23:34) and we know it only too well (Pars I, caput V, Quaest. XI). In the same way and for the same reason, "the Jews should not be presented as repudiated or cursed by God, as if such views followed from the holy Scriptures" (*Nostra Aetate,* 4), even though it is true that "the Church is the new people of God" (ibid.).

V. THE LITURGY

23. Jews and Christians find in the Bible the very substance of their liturgy: for the proclamation of God's word, response to it, prayer of praise and intercession for the living and the dead, recourse to the divine mercy. The Liturgy of the word in its own structure originates in Judaism. The prayer of Hours and other liturgical texts and formularies have their parallels in Judaism as do the very formulas of our most venerable prayers, among them the Our Father. The eucharistic prayers also draw inspiration from models in the Jewish tradition. As John Paul II said (Allocution of March 6th, 1982): ". . . the faith and religious life of the Jewish people as they are professed and practised still today, can greatly help us to understand better certain aspects of the life of the Church. Such is the case of liturgy. . . ."

24. This is particularly evident in the great feasts of the liturgical year, like the Passover. Christians and Jews celebrate the Passover: the Jews, the historic Passover looking towards the future; the Christians, the Passover accomplished in the death and resurrection of Christ, although still in expectation of the final consummation (cf. *supra* no. 9). It is still the "memorial" which comes to us from the Jewish tradition, with a specific content different in each case. On either side, however, there is a like dynamism: for Christians it gives meaning to the eucharistic celebration (cf. the antiphon *O sacrum convivium*), a paschal celebration and as such a making present of the past, but experienced in the expectation of what is to come.

VI. JUDAISM AND CHRISTIANITY IN HISTORY

25. The history of Israel did not end in 70 A.D. (cf. *Guidelines,* II). It continued, especially in a numerous Diaspora which allowed Israel to carry to the whole world a witness—often heroic—of its fidelity to the

one God and to "exalt Him in the presence of all the living" (Tobit 13:4), while preserving the memory of the land of their forefathers at the heart of their hope (Passover *Seder*).

Christians are invited to understand this religious attachment which finds its roots in Biblical tradition, without however making their own any particular religious interpretation of this relationship (cf. *Declaration* of the U.S. Conference of Catholic Bishops, November 20, 1975).

The existence of the State of Israel and its political options should be envisaged not in a perspective which is in itself religious, but in their reference to the common principles of international law.

The permanence of Israel (while so many ancient peoples have disappeared without trace) is a historic fact and a sign to be interpreted within God's design. We must in any case rid ourselves of the traditional idea of a people *punished,* preserved as a *living argument* for Christian apologetic. It remains a chosen people, "the pure olive on which were grafted the branches of the wild olive which are the gentiles" (John Paul II, 6th March, 1982, alluding to Rm 11:17–24). We must remember how much the balance of relations between Jews and Christians over two thousand years has been negative. We must remind ourselves how the permanence of Israel is accompanied by a continuous spiritual fecundity, in the rabbinical period, in the Middle Ages and in modern times, taking its start from a patrimony which we long shared, so much so that "the faith and religious life of the Jewish people as they are professed and practised still today, can greatly help us to understand better certain aspects of the life of the Church" (John Paul II, March 6th, 1982). Catechesis should on the other hand help in understanding the meaning for the Jews of the extermination during the years 1939–1945, and its consequences.

26. Education and catechesis should concern themselves with the problem of racism, still active in different forms of anti-Semitism. The Council presented it thus: "Moreover, (the Church) mindful of her common patrimony with the Jews and motivated by the Gospel's spiritual love and by no political considerations, deplores the hatred, persecutions and displays of anti-Semitism directed against the Jews at any time and from any source" (*Nostra Aetate,* 4). The *Guidelines* comment: "The spiritual bonds and historical links binding the Church to Judaism condemn (as opposed to the very spirit of Christianity) all forms of anti-Semitism and discrimination, which in any case the dignity of the human person alone would suffice to condemn" (*Guidelines,* Preamble).

CONCLUSION

27. Religious teaching, catechesis and preaching should be a preparation not only for objectivity, justice, tolerance but also for understanding and dialogue. Our two traditions are so related that they cannot ignore each other. Mutual knowledge must be encouraged at every level. There is evident in particular a painful ignorance of the history and traditions of Judaism, of which only negative aspects and often caricature seem to form part of the stock ideas of many Christians.

That is what these notes aim to remedy. This would mean that the Council text and *Guidelines and Suggestions* would be more easily and faithfully put into practice.

JOHANNES CARDINAL WILLEBRANDS
President

PIERRE DUPREY
Vice-President

JORGE MEJÍA
Secretary

III.
STATEMENTS ON
CATHOLIC-JEWISH RELATIONS

1. A Note for the Presentation of the Document of the Commission for Religious Relations with the Jews [Notes on the Correct Way to Present the Jews and Judaism in Preaching and Catechesis in the Roman Catholic Church]

Jorge Mejia

The document published here is the result of long and considered work by our Commission.

At the beginning of March 1982, delegates of episcopal conferences and other experts met in Rome to examine a first draft. It was in the course of preparations for this meeting that requests from various quarters came to the Commission, asking that a guide be prepared. Such a guide would be for the use of all those in the Church who have the difficult task of presenting Jews and Judaism to the Catholic faithful in the light of new pastoral and doctrinal developments. These developments flow from the conciliar Declaration *Nostra Aetate,* 4, published twenty years ago and also from the *Guidelines and Suggestions for Implementing the Conciliar Declaration "Nostra Aetate"* (no. 4), published by our Commission at the end of 1974.

The idea was to be of help to those engaged in catechetical work, in teaching and also in preaching, and to put into practice the new directions just mentioned, which are not always easy to translate into teaching methods.

The preparatory work went on for three years. There were several consultations with our consultors in Rome and elsewhere, resulting in several subsequent drafts. Clearly, throughout these stages of the work, and above all in the final one, the drafters kept well in mind what the Holy Father has had to say on Jewish-Catholic relations. He has addressed this subject on various important occasions, from Paris to Mainz, from Brooklyn to Caracas and Madrid, and many times in Rome itself. Neither could the drafters forget the various documents published in recent years by several episcopal conferences. And, at the same time, the Commission along with these consultors and experts took into account the accumulated experience of many years of nearly daily contact with our Jewish partners. For all of that, the text is and remains a document of the Catholic Church. This means that its language, its structure, and the questions it intends to address belong to the teaching and pastoral practice of the Catholic Church.

As is normal procedure with any document published by a department of the Holy See, other departments with competency in the subject matter were consulted. Their observations have been dutifully and carefully taken into account. It is both our duty and our pleasure to express our gratitude and appreciation publicly to them for their patient and fruitful collaboration with us.

The document, in this its final version, bears the title *Notes on the Correct Way to Present the Jews and Judaism in Preaching and Catechesis in the Roman Catholic Church*. The first word of the title (*Notes*) appropriately indicates the *aim* of the text. It is intended to provide a helpful frame of reference for those who are called upon in various ways in the course of their teaching assignments to speak about Jews and Judaism and who wish to do so in keeping with the current teaching of the Church in this area. As everyone knows, this happens quite often. In fact, it is a practical impossibility to present Christianity while abstracting from the Jews and Judaism, unless one were to suppress the Old Testament, forget about the Jewishness of Jesus and the Apostles, and dismiss the vital cultural and religious context of the primitive Church. Neither is it an alternative to present one and the other in a prejudiced, unfavorable light. It is precisely this way of acting that the Council wanted to put an end to. That was also the aim that the 1974 *Guidelines* addressed more or less on the level of general principles. It is exactly the same aim that the present *Notes* address on a more concrete level—one might almost say in handbook style, as long as one keeps in mind the limitations of a text that cannot and should not be too lengthy.

Hence, the *structure* of the document. It starts with a series of "Preliminary Considerations," which introduce the spirit and the rationale of the text, mostly with the help of quotations from the Council, the Holy Father, or from preceding documents. Thereupon follows a *first section* called "Religious Teaching and Judaism," in which the doctrinal and pastoral principles underlying such teaching are set forth. Of special note is paragraph no. 3, which speaks about Judaism as a present reality and not only as a "historical" (and thus superseded) reality. Also to be noted is no. 5 on the complexity of both the historical and the religious relationships between the Church and Judaism. In this same section there is an affirmation that is important for the Catholic Church concerning the centrality of Christ and his unique value in the economy of salvation (no. 7). Clearly this does not mean, however, that the Jews cannot and should not draw salvific gifts from their own traditions. Of course, they can, and should do so.

A *second section* is entitled "Relations between the Old and New Testament." This tries to help put into practice the directions of the Second Vatican Council that call for providing the Catholic faithful with access to a fuller and richer knowledge of Holy Scripture (cf. *Dei Verbum,* 21–22 and *Sacrosanctum Concilium,* 51). This especially includes the Old Testament. It is not always an easy matter to present the relations between both Testaments in a way that fully respects the validity of the Old Testament and shows its permanent usefulness for the Church. At this point, an effort is made to explain the meaning of what is called "typology," since on this a large part of our liturgical use of the Old Testament is grounded. In no way is "typological" usage a devaluation of the validity proper to the Old Testament. Rather to the contrary. One can see this from another angle, since it has always been taught in the Catholic tradition that there is also a "typological" use of the New Testament with respect to the "last things" or eschatological realities (cf. no. 16). The importance of the Old Testament for Judaism is underlined. So, too, is the importance of Jews and Christians hearing the Old Testament together, so that together, in the path opened by the prophetic tradition, we may become more deeply engaged as fellow partisans for humanity today (no. 18, 19). The significance of the continuity of the Jewish people in history is again mentioned toward the end of this document (cf. no. 33). It should also be noted that the limits of "typological" usage are acknowledged, and other possible ways of reading the Old Testament in relation to the New are not excluded (cf. no. 11).

The *third section* speaks about the "Jewish Roots of Christianity." Here we turn to the New Testament and try to show that the Jewishness of Jesus and the Judaism of his time are far from being something marginal or incidental. On the contrary, they are connected with the very dynamic of the Incarnation. Thus, they have a specific value in the divine plan of salvation. The relationship of Jesus to the biblical law is carefully assessed (no. 21). So, too, are his relations to the Jewish religious institutions of his time, including the Temple (no. 22). Also carefully assessed are his contacts with the Pharisees, who constituted a movement within the Judaism of his time with which, beyond doubt, he had very close relations and to which he was very near—notwithstanding appearances to the contrary, about which more is said in the subsequent section.

This *fourth section* is, in fact, given over to the problem of the way "The Jews in the New Testament" are presented. On the basis of an exceedingly superficial analysis, some (Jews and Christians) feel that the New Testament is "anti-Semitic." By contrast, in this document the sound and proven results of recent scholarly exegesis are taken into account. Relying on this evidence, principles and criteria are offered to teachers for the presentation and explanation of texts that can create difficulty, whether these are found in the Gospel of John or in other New Testament writings. There is no intention, however, of hiding the fact of the disbelief of Jews in Jesus, a fact which is here called "sad," just as it is in the well-known text of the Letter to the Romans (9:2). In fact, it is also from this point that the division and enmity between Christians and Jews originated, and it is also from this fact that the present urgent need for reconciliation derives, as is very carefully noted (cf. no. 29 D). At the same time, with no less care, it is emphasized that no one can judge the conscience of another, neither of others in the past nor—still less—of others today (ibid., E, F). In this connection, the teaching of the Second Vatican Council on religious liberty must constantly be kept in mind, since this is "one of the bases on which rests the Jewish-Christian dialogue promoted by the Council" (ibid., F). A special paragraph is dedicated to the "delicate question of responsibility for the death of Christ" (no. 30). No attempt is made, however, to enter into complex and difficult historical questions. Rather, in keeping with the viewpoint of the Catechism of the Council of Trent (here quoted explicitly), the text focuses on the theological significance of the death of Christ and our participation in it as sinners. From this perspective, the historical role of "those few Jews" and those few Romans in Jesus' passion becomes a very secondary matter. (The Creed of the Catholic Church has always mentioned Pontius Pilate in relation with the death of Christ, not the Jews).

In the *fifth section,* reference is made to the liturgy and to similarities and points of contact with Jewish worship. Specific mention is made of the source of our prayers, of the cycle of feasts, and of the very structure itself of our eucharistic prayers.

A *sixth section* contains material altogether new in this series of documents. It intends to offer some information on the common history of Judaism and Christianity down through the centuries, a history that unfortunately is largely unknown or poorly understood if not altogether distorted. In this section, the central elements are chiefly three. First, the permanence of Judaism and, as we say, its theological significance, "which allowed Israel to carry to the whole word a witness—often heroic —of its fidelity to the one God" (no. 33). Second, the "religious attachment" of the Jews to the "land of their forefathers," which Christians are encouraged to try to understand (ibid.). And third, the creation of the State of Israel. This is taken up with extreme precision. It is said that the "perspective" in which the State should be "envisaged" is not "in itself religious." It should be seen "in . . . reference to the common principles of international law" which govern the existence of the various states and their place in the community of nations (ibid.). It will surely be noted that for the first time in a document of this Commission, in different but related paragraphs, reference is made to the land and the State. A brief sentence at the end of the paragraph refers to the "extermination" of the Jews (in Hebrew, the *Shoah,* i.e., the catastrophe) during the dark years of the Nazi persecution. It calls upon Catholics to understand how decisive such a tragedy was for the Jews, a tragedy that is also obviously ours. Several teaching aids have been prepared, including those by Catholic offices for education, to help Catholics better comprehend the senseless dimensions of this tragedy and to grasp better its significance. Our Commission is gratified by these efforts and, with this brief emphasis, would like to indicate in them the path to be followed.

Here again (cf. no. 34), as well as toward the beginning of the document (cf. no. 8), the text repeats its condemnation of anti-Semitism. This time, however, that condemnation is explicit linked with the necessity of a "precise, objective, and rigorously accurate teaching on Judaism," which is the aim of these *Notes.* We are well aware that much has been done to dispel what has been called the "teaching of contempt" (the expression comes from the famous Jewish historian from France, Jules Isaac). But much still remains to be done, not least because new forces of racism and anti-Semitism remain ever ready to rise.

The aim of the *Notes* is, thus, a thoroughly positive one, as the "Conclusion" states. They seek to promote the formation of Catholics equipped "not only for objectivity, justice, and tolerance" (which would already mean a lot), but "also for understanding dialogue". Indeed, "our two traditions are so related that they cannot ignore each other (as is still frequently the case)." It remains a constant necessity that "mutual knowledge . . . be encouraged at every level."

It is our hope that the in-depth study of this text can be carried out by both parties in an atmosphere free of preconceptions and attentive to meaning and sometimes delicate nuances of many paragraphs. This will help us towards our highly desired goal, which is also the indispensable condition for our united and truly efficacious action together in behalf of the ideals we hold dear and which we have inherited from our shared biblical tradition.

> MONSIGNOR JORGE MEJÍA
> *Secretary*
> *Commission for Religious Relations with the Jews*

Rome, June 24, 1985
(Translated from the Italian)

2. Within Context: Guidelines for the Catechetical Presentation of Jews and Judaism in the New Testament [1986]

Secretariat for Catholic-Jewish Relations, NCCB;
Adult Education Department, USCC;
Interfaith Affairs Department, ADL

GUIDELINES FOR TEACHERS

What follows is meant to provide insight and direction for catechists, homilists and textbook publishers in their presentation of the subjects treated. It is hoped that they will help to correct misunderstandings, enlarge vision and, through proper interpretation of the New Testament text in its fuller context, point to deeper interfaith understanding between Christians and Jews today.

HISTORICAL PERSPECTIVES

The Jewishness of Jesus

Jesus was born, lived and died a Jew of his times. He, his family and all his original disciples followed the laws, traditions and customs of his people. The key concepts of Jesus' teaching, therefore, cannot be understood apart from the Jewish heritage. Even after the Resurrection, Jesus' followers understood and articulated the Christ Event through essentially Jewish categories drawn from Jewish tradition and liturgical practice. An appreciation of Judaism in Second Temple times is essential for an adequate understanding of Jesus' mission and teaching, and therefore that of the Church itself.

Jewish Society in Jesus' Time

The Judaism into which Jesus was born and in which the early Church developed was characterized by a multiplicity of interpretation of the Scriptures and of Jewish tradition. These combined with external cultural and political pressures, such as the attractiveness of Hellenism and the heavy burden of Roman occupation, to lead to the formation of numerous sects and movements. Such groups included the *Sadducees,* who were closely associated with the Temple priesthood, held to a literal interpretation of the Bible and tended to cooperate with Roman rule; various groups of *Pharisees,* who developed a uniquely flexible mode of interpreting Scripture and held doctrines opposed by the Sadducees; *Essenes,* who strove for a life of abstinence and purity in a communal setting and viewed the established Temple priesthood as violating the Torah's sacrificial law (among the Essenes would seem to be the authors of the Dead Sea Scrolls); various other apocalyptic circles, who felt the End was near and the redemption of Israel from foreign oppression at hand; revolutionary movements such as the *Zealots,* who advocated violent rebellion against Rome; and various political groupings, such as the *Herodians,* who were supporters of the existing political situation and collaborators with Rome. Given the pressure of Roman occupation, these movements existed in a state of flux and tension rather than as neatly discrete groups.

Pharisees and Sadducees

The Pharisees and Sadducees are the two groups perhaps most frequently mentioned in the gospels, often as Jesus' opponents in particular debates. Here, it is important to emphasize that these groups were quite often at odds with one another and, especially in the case of the Pharisees, often divided among themselves on key issues as well.

In Jesus' lifetime the Pharisees were a popularly based lay group, whose main concern was bringing the people as a whole to a level of sanctity and observance of the Torah then understood as being virtually equivalent to that expected of the Temple priesthood. The Sadducees, allied with the aristocracy and the Temple hierarchy, rejected the innovative interpretations of Scripture offered by the Pharisees and understood religious observance to be defined by literal adherence to the written text of the Bible.

The gospel portrayal of the Pharisees and Sadducees is influenced by the theological concerns of the Evangelists at the time the texts were set in writing some generations after Jesus' death. Many New Testament references hostile or less than favorable to Jews and Judaism actually have their historical context in conflicts between local Christian and Jewish communities in the last decades of the first century (*Notes*, IV). Gospel depictions of conflict between Jesus and groups such as the Pharisees often reflect the deterioration of Christian-Jewish relations in this later period, long after the time of Jesus. So it is at times difficult to ascertain Jesus' actual relations with these groups.

Still, some things are known which drastically change the traditional understanding of Jesus' relationship with the Pharisees. First, his teachings are closer to those of the Pharisees than to those of any other group of the period, and relatively distant from the biblical literalism that characterized the Sadducees. Secondly, the Pharisees were known to be divided among themselves on key issues, principally between the followers of Beth Hillel and those of Beth Shammai. The latter generally took a more strict interpretation of the law and the former a more lenient approach, from what we know of the two movements from later rabbinic materials. Jesus' interpretations, in the main, would appear to have been closer in spirit to those ascribed by later tradition to the "House" of Hillel. Certain of the conflicts between Jesus and "the Pharisees" as depicted in the New Testament then, may well reflect *internal* Pharisaic disputes, with Jesus siding with one "side" against the other.

Jewish Roots of Christian Teaching and Worship

Despite the difficulties of historical reconstruction, however, we can say with some degree of certainty that Jesus shared with the majority of Jews of his time a deep reverence for the Torah. Further, his teaching had much in common with teachings distinctive to the Pharisees in the period, for example belief in the resurrection of the dead, emphasis on the love of God and neighbor, expectation of the coming Kingdom of God and a final judgment, the importance of both humility before and trust in God, and the confidence to pray to God as a loving Father (*Notes* III). Likewise, the early Church organized its communal life and worship principally on Jewish liturgical models such as that of the synagogue (*Notes* V). Hence, Christian liturgy itself cannot be understood without reference to ongoing Jewish practice and tradition, both biblical and postbiblical (See *Sacramental Preparation* and *Catechesis and Liturgy* below).

CATECHETICAL PRINCIPLES

The Gospels and the Hebrew Scriptures

It is essential to remember that the gospels represent theological reflections on the life and teaching of Jesus which, while historically based, were not intended by their authors to be eyewitness accounts. Indeed, the gospels were set down in final form some 40 to 70 years after Jesus' death. Thus they reflect a long and complex editorial process (*Notes* IV). In their final form they make use of a variety of literary genres, styles, and rhetorical devices common to the Jewish culture of the times.

Using methods familiar to us from contemporary Jewish apocalyptic and Essene writings (e.g., the Dead Sea Scrolls), as well as early rabbinic literature, the New Testament authors sought to explain their experience of Jesus in terms of their Jewish heritage, especially by using passages from the Hebrew Scriptures. When reading the prophets (e.g., Isaiah 7:14, 52–53; Hosea 11:1; Micah 5:1), the Evangelists interpreted Jewish hopes for deliverance as foretelling Jesus' coming. *Such post-Resurrection insights do not replace the original intentions of the prophets.* Nor does Christian affirmation of the validity of the Evangelists' insight preclude the validity of post-New Testament and present Jewish insight into the meaning of prophetic texts (*Notes* I, II). It can easily be seen, however, how use of the same symbols with different meanings can give rise to misunderstandings and even resentment between Jews and Christians today.

The Second Vatican Council clearly taught that God's covenant with and therefore presence among the Jewish people as God's own people has not been abrogated by the coming of Christ: "now as before, God holds the Jews most dear for the sake of their fathers; He does not repent of the gifts he makes or of the calls He issues" (*Nostra Aetate,* No. 4). Thus post-New Testament, rabbinic Jewish insight into the meaning of the Hebrew Scriptures, which Jews and Christians share, retains its own validity. With discerning respect for the differences between Jewish and Christian readings of the Bible, Christian catechesis can and should profit immeasurably from the traditions of Jewish biblical interpretation and spiritual insight.

Jewish Religious Traditions

Since Jewish tradition provides the context not only for Jesus' message but also for the development of the early Church, an awareness of this ongoing heritage is essential for an adequate Christian catechesis. This heritage, it is important to emphasize, involves not simply biblical Judaism, but rabbinic and present-day Jewish religious life as well. Just as each successive generation of Christians has reaffirmed and thereby "made its own" the Apostolic witness preserved in the New Testament, so each generation of Jews has continued to carry on Israel's ancient dialogue with God. Thus, in presenting the early Church's witness as a living reality pertinent to contemporary life, catechists do well to present also the living witness of the Jewish people to God's enduring fidelity to His covenant with them (*Notes,* VI). A tiny sampling of the spiritual riches pertinent to catechesis in ongoing Jewish tradition is given here in the hope of motivating further and deeper study of Judaism among Catholic religious educators.

The Nature of God

In Judaism, God is seen as the Lord of history, extending justice to all men and women, and as a loving, merciful parent fulfilling both paternal and maternal roles. Rabbinic commentary interprets God's Name in Exodus 34:6–7 as "thirteen names for mercy." God is both transcendent and immanent, King and Father, worshiped in awe yet close enough to "pitch his tent" with His people.

Jewish Ethics

Jewish ethics are marked by a sense of "imitation of God," from its understanding of Creation (Gen. 1:27) to its understanding of Covenant ("Be holy as I the Lord your God am holy," Lev. 19:2). The Jewish Law of Love, reaffirmed by Jesus, finds its source and fuller context in the Pentateuch (Dt. 6:5; Lev. 19:18, 33–34), as do the works of mercy (Lev. 19; Dt. 9:10–19), forgiveness of one who has wronged you and even the feeding of one's enemy (Ex. 23:4; Prov. 25:21–22). Rabbinic commentaries on these and similar biblical passages (e.g., on the need for repentance) can add depth of insight and a challenging concreteness to classroom discussion. On the basis of imitating God, for example, rabbinic commentary has expounded on the works of mercy: "He (God) clothes the naked. . . . You, too, should clothe the naked! The Holy One, praised be He, visited the sick. . . . You, too, should visit the sick!" (B. Sotah 14a). Rabbinic writings on the need to imitate God's forgiveness are numerous: "Rabbi Gamaliel said: Let this be a sign to you, that whenever you are compassionate, the Compassionate One will have compassion on you." (T. Bab. K. ix, 29, 30); "Be merciful on earth, as our Father in heaven is merciful" (Targ. Jerus. I. Lev. 22.28).

Pope John Paul II, during his historic visit to the Rome Synagogue, stated that Jews and Christians are, together, "the trustees and witnesses of an ethic marked by the Ten Commandments, in the observance of which humanity finds truth and freedom. To promote a common reflection and collaboration on this point is one of the great duties of the hour."

The Jewish Sense of Mission

The Jewish sense of mission is expressed in the prophets Isaiah, Jeremiah, Ezekiel and in later prayers from medieval and modern times as "the hallowing of God's name" throughout the world. It is a call to see that God's Name is known, and praised by, all the nations of the earth. This belief that God should be honored by all humanity is developed in the rabbinic idea that God's Covenant with Noah (as distinct from the one with Abraham) is a universal covenant and a means by which all people can be brought to salvation. This universal concept underlies Judaism's vision of God's Kingdom as a time when all nations will come to worship on the holy mountain, and will gather from the East and from the West to sit down together at God's holy banquet (e.g., Isaiah, Micah, etc.). The Jewish sense of mission has resulted in many martyrs, not only in biblical times, as reflected in the books of the Maccabees, but during Christian times as well, for example during the Crusades, when thousands of Jews died rather than abandon their faith. This "heroic witness" of the Jewish people through history (Notes VI) needs to be acknowledged and honored today. It is, finally, part of Jewish belief that when the divine Name is praised throughout the world, God's Kingdom will be fulfilled.

Jewish Understanding of God's Reign

The Jewish understanding of God's reign is of universal harmony and wholeness (shalom), in which all the peoples of the earth will gather to worship God. This understanding of the End toward which all human history is oriented provides a constant and present challenge to Christians and Jews (e.g., Isaiah 2:11; 25; 35; Micah 4:4).

Jewish Prayer and Liturgy

Jewish prayer—like Jewish ethics—is structured upon the idea of correspondence between heaven and earth. It is, accordingly, divided into two parts of ascending and descending blessings: the worshiper first offers praise to God, naming a special attribute, then asks for blessings which correspond to that quality. The great prayer of Jesus (the "Our Father") is characteristic of Jewish prayer not only in terms of its special phrasing (every line of the Our Father is paralleled in the Jewish prayer book, *Siddur*) but also in terms of structure. The first part of the prayer consists of ascending blessings in which God is praised as a Father. The worshiper expresses the missionary longing for the honoring of His Name and the coming of His Kingdom. In the second part of the prayer, the worshiper asks for those descending blessings appropriate for God as a Father to bestow: bread, forgiveness, deliverance. In between the two parts is a "hinge" line expressing the desire for correspondence between heaven and earth.

The desire for this correspondence between heaven and earth permeates the Sabbath liturgy, which invariably begins with the same motifs of praise of God and longing for His Kingdom. In rabbinic interpretation, the Sabbath laws are said to anticipate the Kingdom by freeing every creature from ordinary work (even beasts) and banning even the mention of sickness, death, and war. The harmony of the universe at the moment of Creation is recalled and extolled as God's purpose. The seventh day of peace (the Sabbath) is thus seen as the end of time as well as the beginning. The theme of this total peace (*shabbat shalom*) dominates the liturgy. This sense of wholeness and unity is intended to mark both the hearing of God's word in the synagogue and the festive Sabbath meal in the home. The Sabbath afternoon prayers recognize, however, that this perfect state has not yet arrived by concluding with the pilgrim psalms: an acknowledgment that humanity is not yet arrived at Jerusalem, is still on a journey to the holy society.

The great Jewish festivals underscore in different ways this constant journeying toward wholeness: Passover (*Pesach*), which celebrates the deliverance from bondage and the movement toward the Promised Land; Pentecost (*Shevuoth*), which celebrates the giving of the Torah, God's Word seen as the source of life, a bridge between His transcendent being and His indwelling presence; and *Succoth* or Tabernacles, which is a Festival of Thanksgiving, a Feast of Ingathering. The solemn feasts of New Year and Atonement (*Rosh Hashanah* and *Yom Kippur*) acknowl-

edge this journeying as the human condition and express it in the realities
of human sin and repentance, divine justice and forgiving love.

Torah and Gospel

While the Jewish term, *Torah,* is usually rendered in English translations as "Law," a more accurate rendering of the Hebrew would be
"Teaching" or "Instruction." In Judaism, *Torah* is the term used to
identify the Pentateuch and by extension the whole of the Jewish "Way"
of life in covenant with God (*Halakah*). Torah is thus understood as the
revealed will of God, the response God expects of the people whom He
has saved and with whom He has entered into an eternal, unbreakable
covenant.

Jesus and the Torah

Jesus lived by this Torah and even entered into disputes concerning
its meaning. The authority of Jesus' person and the uniqueness of his
teaching are highlighted in the gospel texts, and certain of the gospel
accounts of disputes between Jesus and his fellow Jews appear to revolve
around the authority Jesus claimed for himself as *interpreter* of Torah.

Jesus accepted and observed the Law (cf. Gal. 4:4; Lk. 2:21–24),
extolled respect for it, and invited obedience to it (Mt. 5:17–20). Therefore, it can never be valid to place Jesus' teaching (gospel) in fundamental
opposition to the Torah. The dynamic reality that is Jewish Law should
never be depicted as "fossilized" or reduced to "legalism." This would be
to misread and absolutize certain New Testament polemical passages
apart from their particular context and intent. (See *Pharisees and Sadducees* and *The Gospels and the Hebrew Scriptures* above.)

Saint Paul and the Law

While Saint Paul argued that the Law was not binding on Gentiles
who had been admitted to the covenant through what God had accomplished in Jesus, he never suggested that the Law (*Torah*) had ceased to be
God's will for the Jewish people. In Romans 9–11, Paul reveals his deep
love for his people (9:3), and insists that God has by no means rejected
the Jews (11:1–2). Regarding the Jews and the Torah, Paul states that
even after the founding of the Church, the relationship is enduring and
valid, for "God's gifts and call are irrevocable" (11:29). Even though God

has shown His Mercy in allowing Gentiles to become "the children of God" in Christ (9:6–18), Paul's "kin according to the flesh, the Israelites," possess "the adoption, the glory, the covenants, the law-giving, the worship and the promises" (9:4; cf. 1975 NCCB Statement on Catholic-Jewish Relations).

Catechetical Goal

Catechesis should make clear the sense of "partnership" in God's plan that should prevail in all relations between Jews and Christians. The process of catechesis, in the words of the Vatican *Notes,* is to bring students to "a greater awareness that the people of God of the Old and the New Testament are tending toward a like end in the future: the coming or return of the Messiah—even if they start from two different points of view. Transmitted early enough by catechesis, such a conception will teach young Christians in a practical way to cooperate with Jews, going beyond even dialogue" (*Notes* II, 10–11).

Presentation of Jesus' Passion

It is crucial for catechesis to provide a proper context for understanding the death of Jesus. Like the New Testament as a whole, the Passion narratives of the four gospels are not entirely eyewitness accounts of the historical events, but later, post-Resurrection reflections from different perspectives on the meaning of Jesus' death and resurrection. Common to all accounts is the core gospel message that Jesus died "because of the sins of all, so that all might attain salvation." (*Nostra Aetate,* No. 4). Any explanation which directly or implicitly imputes collective responsibility on the Jewish people for Jesus' death not only obscures this central truth, but can also lead to anti-Semitism.

Reconstructing the Events of Jesus' Death

Biblical scholarship cannot at present reconstruct with full confidence all of the historical events surrounding Jesus' death. All four gospels, however, reveal a striking similarity in certain essentials: Last Supper with the disciples, betrayal by Judas, arrest in an outdoor area outside the city (because the authorities feared Jesus' popularity with his fellow Jews), interrogation before a high priest, appearance before and condemnation by Pontius Pilate, being led off to death at the hands of Roman soldiers, crucifixion, title on the cross ("King of the Jews"), death, burial, and resurrection. These details provide a level of agreement among the Evangelists practically unique in the Jesus story.

Certain differences of detail reflect the individual author's or redactor's own views from the time in which the narrative was set down. Comparison of the various gospel accounts of the Passion can help the teacher to understand what is particular to a given author and what pertains to the essence of the gospels' common understanding of Jesus' death and resurrection. For example, the phrase, "and all the people shouted back, his blood be on us and on our children," is cited only in Matthew 27:25, while both Mark and Luke distinguish between the "small crowd" before Pilate and "the people," who sympathize with Jesus (e.g., Luke 23:27).

Neither John nor Luke record a formal Sanhedrin "trial" of Jesus, making such a scene historically uncertain. Likewise there is a tendency from the earlier gospels (especially Mark) to the later (Matthew and John) to place more and more of the onus on "the Jews" and less on Pilate, who alone had the authority to order a crucifixion (John 18:31), a notion emphasized in Matthew's hand-washing scene (Mt. 27:24). The use of the general term, "the Jews" in the Passion narrative of the Gospel of John can lead to a sense of collective guilt if not carefully explained.

Such scenes, transmitted uncritically in the classroom, can lead to misunderstanding of the nature of New Testament narrative and even to anti-Jewish hostility among students, as history has shown all too well. Therefore, a careful attempt to contextualize passages describing conflict between Jesus and various Jewish groups is essential in catechesis today.

The Pharisees and the Crucifixion

The Pharisees should not be depicted as implacable opponents of Jesus. They shared with him much that was central to his teaching. Moreover, the Passion accounts do not mention the Pharisees as playing a significant role in Jesus' death. One passage, Luke 13:31, even tells us that Pharisees tried to warn Jesus of a Herodian plot against his life.

The Role of Pilate

Educators need to stress what is known from extrabiblical material about the oppressive nature of Roman rule in Judea and about Pilate's unsavory historical character. The Roman governor appointed the high priests of the Temple and could depose them at will. Thus, Pilate would have been in control of the situation throughout the events of Jesus' arrest and crucifixion. Pilate is known to have been a particularly strong and cruel procurator. He crucified hundreds of Jews without recourse to Jewish or Roman law. Among them, as we know from the gospels, was Jesus. Pilate was eventually recalled by Rome to account for his cruelties and the unrest in the Jewish population that they precipitated. The Creed, it should be recalled, mentions only Pilate in connection with Jesus' death, not Jews.

The modern experience of oppressed peoples under totalitarian occupation—from France under the Nazis to Afghanistan under the Soviets—may be utilized for an understanding of the tensions between collaborators and patriots.

Catechetical Goal

The central focus of catechesis should be on the theological significance of the events and on our own participation in it as sinners (Catechism of the Council of Trent). The above principles are especially important in catechesis preparing for Lent and Holy Week (*Notes* IV).

CATECHETICAL PRACTICES

Maturity in Faith as Catechetical Goal

Fostering maturity in faith is the central task of catechesis, at the earliest age and continuing through life in ways appropriate to the growth of the believer. Mature faith involves the fullest understanding of one's spiritual identity and the fullest respect for the spiritual identity of another. To understand their own identity, Christians need to know and appreciate their rootedness in biblical Judaism. They need to recognize and accept the fact that Jesus was a devout Jew, and so cherish the Jewish traditions they have inherited through him. They also need to understand that Rabbinical Judaism developed at the same time as Christianity and that both modern religions are characterized by many similar responses to ancient teachings and customs. If their faith is mature, Christians will not be threatened by dialogue with modern Judaism, but rather, challenged and inspired by its spiritual riches. Mature Christian faith sees itself not as opposing Judaism, but as integrally bound with it in fulfilling God's redemptive plan for the world.

"Attentive to the same God who has spoken, hanging on the same word, we have to witness to one same memory and one common hope in Him who is the master of history" (*Notes,* I, 11).

Sacramental Preparation

While the Catholic definition of a sacrament as "a sign instituted by Christ" might seem to make marginal any reference to Judaism, the reality is that here, as elsewhere in his teaching, Jesus and the early Church drew upon the riches of Jewish tradition. While Jews have never used the vocabulary of "sacrament" as developed in Christian liturgical tradition, the "sacramental view" of life—that Creation is holy and that God speaks and is present to us through material signs—is inherently Jewish.

Signs of God's Presence

A Jewish concept which profoundly implies this "sacramental" view is found in the rabbinic use of the term *shekinah,* a feminine word signifying divine Presence. Numerous biblical stories describe ways in which God becomes present to the chosen people through concrete signs, e.g., the burning bush, the parting of the Red Sea, the cloud and pillar of fire in Exodus, the cloud which filled the Temple at its dedication (1 Kings 8), and the rush of the spirit upon David at the time of his anointing. Connected with such stories of liberation and empowerment are the Jewish rituals of washings (*mikveh*), and anointing. The Christian practice of baptism derives from the Hebrew *mikveh.* Christian practices of anointing reflect the biblical practice of anointing kings and prophets. The Hebrew term "Messiah" means "the anointed one."

Sacramental Theory

In addition to the sacramental perspective and the Jewish origins of Christian ritual, Christian sacramental theory is rooted in Jewish concepts of the biblical and Second Temple periods: that human beings stand in constant need of repentance and atonement for sin; that the religious community may make use of the mediating ritual of priests; and that the commitment of married love is so holy that it can stand as a metaphor for the covenant between God and the people of God.

The Eucharist

The central action of Christian worship—the Eucharist—not only has its origins in the prayers and rituals of the Passover meal (e.g., the blessings over the bread and wine), but takes its essential significance from the Jewish understanding of *Zikkaron* ("memorial re-enactment"), i.e., the concept that God's saving presence is not only recalled but actually re-lived through a ritual meal. The Synoptic Gospels thus imply that Jesus instituted the Eucharist during a Passover *Seder* celebrated with his followers.

Catechesis and Liturgy

A primary task of catechesis is preparation for the liturgy. Here, it can be stressed that both Jews and Christians find in the Bible the very substance of their communal worship: proclamation of and response to God's Word, prayers of praise to God and intercession for the living and the dead, recourse to the divine mercy.

The Liturgical Cycle

The Church's liturgical cycle of feasts parallels that of the Synagogue, and in great part draws its origins and continuing sustenance from it. Both Christians and Jews celebrate the Passover. Jews celebrate the historic *Passover* from slavery to freedom, and look forward to the fulfillment of human history in an age of universal justice and peace (*shalom*) for all humanity at the end of time. Christians celebrate the Passover Exodus accomplished in the death and resurrection of Jesus, likewise awaiting its final consummation at the end of time.

St. Luke describes Jews coming to Jerusalem for the feast of Pentecost, which celebrates the giving of the Torah. Christians celebrate the Jewish feast of Pentecost as the occasion of the giving of the Spirit to the apostles. Both traditions observe periods of fasting and repentance in their annual cycles. The liturgical spirit of Advent and Lent is paralleled by the equivalent (though in many ways profoundly distinct) spirit of *teshuvah* ("turning," repentance) and reconciliation evoked by the High Holy Days culminating in Yom Kippur, the Day of Atonement. Commentary on this feast in the Jewish Daily Prayer Book (the *Siddur*) spells out Jewish belief in free will and "the Evil Inclination," the different levels of sin, and the need for continual confession, remorse and a resolution of amendment.

Spiritual Bonds

Not only the great liturgical cycle but also innumerable details of prayer form and ritual exemplify the "spiritual bond" which the Church shares with the Jewish people in every age. The prayer of hours and other liturgical texts draw their inspiration from Synagogue Judaism and a common Bible (especially the Psalms), as do the formulas of the Church's most venerable prayers, such as the Our Father and other Eucharistic prayers. The offering of bread and wine, for example, is rooted in the Jewish *Berakah* ("Praising"): "Blessed are You, Lord our God, King of the Universe, who brings forth bread from the earth."

As Pope John Paul II stated: "The faith and religious life of the Jewish people, as they are professed and practiced still today, can greatly help us to understand certain aspects of the [liturgical] life of the Church."

Catechist Formation

What is true of catechesis in general is of necessity all the more true of programs designed to prepare catechists. Fostering a positive and accurate appreciation of the Jews as God's people still today and of Judaism as a living witness to God's Name in the world should be an essential and not merely an occasional goal in all program planning (*Notes,* I).

Catechists and all teachers of religion share in a special call to hand on the faith of the Church. Catholic faith and Jewish faith are, in the words of Pope John Paul II, "linked together at the very level of their identity" (Rome, March 6, 1982). It is vital that all programs of catechist formation and teacher training provide the elements of Jewish tradition, not only biblical but rabbinic and spiritual traditions and liturgical practice as well. In this way catechists will be better prepared to foster in the students a "full awareness of the heritage common to Jews and Christians" spoken of by the Pope (ibid.) and to share the richness of that heritage.

That this is a task for Catholic "diocesan and parochial organizations, schools, colleges, universities and especially seminaries" is made clear by the Second Vatican Council's Declaration on the Relationship of the Church to Non-Christians (*Nostra Aetate,* No. 4) and subsequent documents of the Holy See and our own National Conference of Catholic Bishops. It is a task "incumbent upon" teachers and theologians, in the words of the 1975 NCCB Statement on Catholic-Jewish Relations. A rich reservoir of resources for teachers and teacher trainers is already in existence.

Preparation and Evaluation of Textbooks

As Bishop Jorge Mejia, then of the Holy See's Commission for Religious Relations with the Jews, stated in announcing the promulgation of the Vatican *Notes,* "It is, in fact, a practical impossibility to present Christianity while abstracting from the Jews and Judaism, unless one were to suppress the Old Testament (Hebrew Scriptures), forget about the Jewishness of Jesus and the Apostles, and dismiss the vital cultural and religious context of the primitive Church" (*L'Osservatore Romano,* June 24, 1985). To be true to the task of presenting the Church's own "story" and message to the world, one must strive to present Judaism and the Jewish people accurately, fully and positively.

Publishers should be encouraged by the progress made in Christian-Jewish relations since the Council, and by the Council's own mandate, to grasp the opportunity given today to infuse their textbooks, teacher manuals and audio-visuals with materials drawn from the rich spiritual heritage of Judaism. The principles and practices listed briefly above will provide publishers with a handy check list of criteria to give to authors and evaluators of all teaching materials. School texts, prayerbooks and other media should, under competent auspices, continue to be examined in order to remove not only those materials that do not accord with the content and spirit of the Church's teaching, but also those that fail to show Judaism's continuing role in salvation history in a positive light.

Reclaiming the Jewish origins of Christianity, together with a sense of the continuing fruitfulness of the Church's spiritual links with the Jewish people today, can greatly enrich and deepen Christian education.

CONCLUDING REFLECTION

The stress in these guidelines, which are meant to complement rather than replace present Catholic religious education curricula, has been on the "common spiritual patrimony" shared by Christianity and Judaism. This is not meant to diminish the uniqueness of Jesus' message or that of the Church, but rather to deepen that message with an appreciation of its interrelatedness with the ongoing witness of the Jewish people.

Pope John Paul II, addressing the Jewish community in the great synagogue of Rome on April 13, 1986, expressed this vision:

> Jews and Christians are the trustees and witnesses of an ethic marked by the Ten Commandments, in the observance of which humanity finds its truth and freedom. To promote a common reflection and collaboration on this point is one of the great duties of the hour. . . . In doing this, we shall each be faithful to our most sacred commitments and also to that which most profoundly unites and gathers us together: faith in the one God who "loves strangers" and "renders justice to the orphan and the widow" (cf. Dt. 10:18), commanding us too to love and help them (cf. Lev. 19:18–34). Christians have learned this desire of the Lord from the Torah, which you here venerate, and from Jesus, who took to its extreme consequences the love demanded by the Torah. . . . The Jewish religion is not "extrinsic" to us, but in a certain way "intrinsic" to our own religion. With Judaism therefore we have a relationship which we do not have with any other religion. You are our dearly beloved brothers. . . . (*Origins,* April 24, 1986).

IV.
FROM ARGUMENT TO DIALOGUE: *NOSTRA AETATE* TWENTY-FIVE YEARS LATER

From Argument to Dialogue:
Nostra Aetate Twenty-Five Years Later

Leon Klenicki

No person outside Israel knows the mystery of Israel. And no person
outside of Christianity knows the mystery of Christianity. But in their
ignorance they can acknowledge each other in the mystery.[1]
Martin Buber

The Declaration on the Relation of the Church to Non-Christian
Religions, *Nostra Aetate,* promulgated on October 28, 1965, by the Second Vatican Council marked a special moment in the history of the
church and its relation to world religions. For the Jewish observer, Vatican II was a unique religious event. The council, as seen from the outside,
endeavored to witness God by a testimony rooted in the Christian tradition of centuries, but sensitive to the realities of change and human
development. The work of the Council—*aggiornamento,* as it was called
by Pope John XXIII—was to lead to an actualization, an active awareness, of the experience of God and God's presence in the contemporary
Christian historical context.

The *aggiornamento* initiated by the Vatican Council is a process of
inner renewal entailing a reckoning of the soul in relation to other faith
commitments. The council undertook a rethinking of Judaism and the
Jewish people in Catholic theology. Negative Christian attitudes of centuries, the teaching of contempt, the denial of Israel's destiny and vocation, required a reflection going beyond the theological triumphalism of
the church fathers and the ideas of medieval theologians.

Karl Barth, a Vatican II Protestant observer, stressed as basic to any

77

rethinking of Christianity the obligation to comprehend Judaism and Israel's role in God's design.

Israel, God's chosen, existed and exists, witnessing God and the covenantal relationship, despite alienation and historical ostracism which culminated in the Holocaust, a devastating reality of total evil. The Holocaust reminds Christians and Jews of the need to account for the Christian teaching of contempt for Judaism and its weight in the cultural milieu of the Western world that prepared the atmosphere for anti-Semitism in its most extreme manifestation. Though not immediately related to Christian thinking, the paganism of Nazi Germany was fed by the ideological reasoning of anti-Judaism in Christian theology and church pronouncements.

The council's reconsideration of Judaism and the Jewish people formed part of a concern over the very meaning of Christian testimony, a search for the "mystery" of its own faith. *Nostra Aetate* follows this inner examination as it relates to the main religious faith commitments, devoting a separate section to Judaism (IV).

Nostra Aetate was prepared and written by Catholic theologians and religious experts and directed to the Catholic community. The original draft, and particularly the fourth section devoted to Judaism, underwent changes after many discussions. The proposal called forth the expression of profound differences among the bishops attending the council. Conservatively oriented clergy and outside groups tried to obstruct consideration of Judaism altogether, using arguments familiar from medieval disputations. For some groups *Nostra Aetate* served as a pretext to criticize Vatican II and to allow nonreligious organizations, the Arab League, and Arab diplomats, for instance, to attack the interreligious dialogue and the State of Israel. A current of anti-Jewish theology was evident in articles and books—underlining God's rejection of Israel and Jewish involvement in the death of Jesus—distributed openly or clandestinely among the council fathers. A text on deicide, written by Luigi M. Carli, Bishop of Segni, accused the council of "historic distortion." Augustin Cardinal Bea responded with a scholarly document published in *Civiltà Cattolica* IV, 21, on November 6, 1965 (later published in English in *Thought* Spring 1966).

VATICAN II DISCUSSION ON JUDAISM

The discussions at Vatican II entailed a constant dialogue of clarification, involving the expertise of Catholic theologians and specialists as well as Jewish personalities active in the interreligious relationship. One of these, Dr. Joseph L. Lichten, played a central role.[2] As director of the Anti-Defamation League of B'nai B'rith's Department of Intercultural Affairs, he represented the organization in Rome during the days of the council. His sensitivity and knowledge of the Jewish-Catholic dialogue were of particular significance in informing council members on the Jewish point of view regarding the main historical and religious problems in the dialogue. He presented a study-survey conducted for the Anti-Defamation League by the Survey Research Center of the University of California, inspired by Oscar Cohen and directed by Charles Glock and Rodney Stark, published later as *Christian Beliefs and Anti-Semitism*.[3] It has become a classic of socioreligious studies and undoubtedly influenced Vatican Council members.

Joseph L. Lichten pointed out the influence of the deicide charge on American Catholics:

> Perhaps as many as five million American Catholics, out of a total of forty-five million, see the Jews as principally responsible for the death of Jesus, and they are led thereby to a negative assessment of the contemporary Jew. The fact that those who believe and feel this way tend to go to church more frequently, underscores the need for the Catholic Church to intensify its efforts if it hopes to bring all Catholics to the principles of brotherhood which it espouses.[4]

Arthur Gilbert described the impact of the Glock-Stark study at the Vatican Council:

> So troubled were Catholic leaders by this startling revelation of Christian anti-Semitism that the Dutch Documentation Center for the Council volunteered to publish the findings and distributed them to every Council Father, since the debate on the Jewish statement was surely to induce comments. Therefore, on September 17, the findings were placed in the mailbox of each Council father with a note by the Center Director expressing his hope that the document would serve the council, the church, and the lapse between Jews and Christians.[5]

The final council vote on the Declaration showed the church's special concern for this document, which was a turning point in Catholic understanding of Judaism and the Christian-Jewish relationship. In the final ballot on the Declaration as a whole, 221 voted yes, 88 voted no, and 3 votes were void.[6]

JEWISH RESPONSES

The reactions to *Nostra Aetate* within the Jewish community were mixed, ranging from total negativism and prudent criticism to reserved acceptance and enthusiasm. Reservations were expressed about the very fact of the publication of a Catholic document on Judaism and dialogue. It reminded many, particularly after the European experience, of previous pronouncements by the church. Those documents of the past were part of the medieval ecclesiastical environment that resulted in the repeated exclusion of Jews from public and national life. It was felt that the Vatican II Declaration on the Jews might be a modern, more sophisticated version of the *Constitutio Pro Iudaeis,* a bull by Pope Calixtus II (1119–1124). This papal document, which established a pattern of relationships with the Jewish people, served as well as a protective statute at a time of persecution by secular powers.[7]

Caution on *Nostra Aetate* was recommended in the interreligious dialogue by Rabbi Joseph B. Soloveitchik, one of the most brilliant Jewish minds of this century, in his essay "Confrontation." In his recommendations to the Rabbinical Council of America he proposed a dialogue that respected each faith's commitments and avoided any theological discussion. He proposed discussions on humanitarian and cultural endeavors and man's moral values. His categorical resistance to theological dialogue was summed up as follows: "To repeat, we are ready to discuss universal religious problems. We will resist any attempt to debate our private individual commitments."[8]

Rabbi Soloveitchick's critique of theological discussion can be understood in historical terms. The medieval disputes and theological confrontations commanded by Catholic religious leaders, obligated the rabbis to discuss the concept of messiah, or the idea of trinity and defend the Jewish position, independent of a Christian interpretation of the Hebrew Bible. The discussions ended by forced conversion to Catholicism or the expulsion of Jews from the city where those "conversations" took place.

The memory of these past events is still present in Jewish life. But, do the pluralistic reality of the United States, religious liberty and Vatican II actuality, admit the triumphalism of the past? It is very doubtful. Interreligious dialogue requires a respectful interchange of different opinions and experiences. It is a sharing of faith that allows for understanding and the acceptance of the other as a person in covenant with God. Even the consideration of social questions, recommended by Rabbi Soloveitchik as the only form of interfaith discussion, entails background knowledge of the respective religious traditions and theological heritage. Otherwise the discussion is a sociological deliberation rather than a religious spiritual understanding.

Rabbi Eliezer Berkovits bitterly criticized dialogue of any kind, especially in what he considered "the post-Christian era." He wrote:

> There is no reason on earth why Judaism should make itself available to fraternal dialogue with a religion which, by its very premises, declares others to be in error and, from the outset, destroys the basis of the true dialogical situation. . . . We reject the idea of interreligious understanding as immoral because it is an attempt to whitewash the criminal past.[9]

There were, however, many Jewish voices that favored dialogue and stressed the importance of the Jewish-Christian relationship, particularly at that moment in history, after the Holocaust and Vatican II. On the American scene, this attitude resulted in special programs by ecclesiastical organizations and private agencies that devoted time and energy to illustrate to the community at large the spiritual and social transcendence of the interreligious encounter. For this reason, American Catholic opinion on many questions regarding religious freedom and interreligious relations was of decisive influence. Jacob B. Agus summed up the mood of search for knowledge and meaning of those days when he said the dialogue should be "mutually challenging, not necessarily mutually contradictory."[10]

In October, 1974, Pope Paul VI instituted a Vatican "Commission for Religious Relations with the Jews," which in 1975 issued the *Guidelines and Suggestions* for *Implementing the Conciliar Declaration Nostra Aetate (n. 4)*. The document suggested changes in the approach to liturgy, teaching and education, and joint social action.[11] The document was an advance over *Nostra Aetate,* but not in relation to previously published guidelines of episcopal conferences in the United States and Europe.[12] A third document was issued in 1985: *Notes on the Correct Way To Present The Jews and Judaism in Preaching and Catechesis of the Roman Catholic Church.*

NOSTRA AETATE: A JEWISH READING

Nostra Aetate is open to interpretation and committed reading, and that process deepens the dialogue. This was done by Catholics all over the world. The statements of the U.S. National Conference of Catholic Bishops in 1975, of the French Bishops Committee for Relations with Jews in 1973, of the National Commission for Relations between Christians and Jews in Belgium of 1973, of the Catholic Church in the Netherlands of 1970, the Synod of Vienna in 1969, and the Brazilian Bishops in the 80s are attempts to deepen the meaning of the Catholic-Jewish dialogue through encounter and theological reflection.[13]

A Jewish reading of the Vatican Statement requires a respectful consideration of the Catholic faith commitment. This must be done in the perspective of Jewish religious thought and the covenantal relationship, but mindful of the Christian vocation. Certain temptations must be avoided; for instance, total negativism regarding the possibilities and future of the dialogue, based on past experiences. Another is self-pity for past persecutions and pains; those were very real events, unfortunate parts of Christian history. But self-righteousness is not an answer to the challenge of dialogue, one of the most difficult challenges to a religious person. The right Jewish attitude in this situation requires self-searching and a spirit of reconciliation. It entails recognition of the dialogue partner as a subject of faith, a child of God. It also calls for a perception of Christianity's role in bringing God's covenant to humanity following the obligation placed upon Noah, the biblical symbol for humankind. Through dialogue, Christianity must overcome the triumphalism of power, Judaism the triumphalism of pain.[14]

Nostra Aetate (no. 4) begins with an explanation of the relationship of the church to Judaism, referred to in the document as "Abraham's stock." The church acknowledges that, according to God's saving design, the beginnings of Christian faith and election "are found already among the patriarchs, Moses and the prophets." All who believe in Christ "are included in the same patriarch's call, and likewise that the salvation of the church is mysteriously foreshadowed by the chosen people's exodus from the land of bondage." The church cannot forget that "she draws sustenance from the root of that well-cultivated olive tree onto which has been grafted the wild shoot, the Gentiles. Indeed, the church believes that by his cross Christ, our Peace, reconciled Jews and Gentiles, making both one in himself."

This terminology is open to misunderstandings, recalling the typological theology which was the basis for much of the teaching of contempt that denied Judaism a place in God's plan for redemption. Christian typology stressed the concept that the *Tanakh,* the Hebrew Bible, is merely a preparation for Jesus' coming and mission, and that Israel lost its purpose and meaning in the divine plan.

Nostra Aetate is obscure in its formulation but the Vatican II *Guidelines* of 1975 emphasize the value of the Hebrew Bible by itself:

An effort will be made to acquire a better understanding of whatever in the Old Testament retains its own perpetual value (cf. *Dei Verbum* 14–15), since that has not been cancelled by the later interpretation of the New Testament.

The French bishops' statement of 1973 adds a dimension of understanding that opens new vistas in the relationship:

According to biblical revelation, God himself constituted this people, brought it up, advised it of his plans, concluding with it an eternal covenant (Gn 17:7), and giving it a vocation which St. Paul qualifies as "irrevocable" (Rom 11:29). We are indebted to the Jewish people for the five books of the Law, the prophets, and the other scriptures which complete the message. After having been collected by oral and written tradition, these precepts were received by Christians without, however, dispossessing the Jews.

Even though in Jesus Christ the covenant was renewed for Christendom, the Jewish people must not be looked upon by Christians as a mere social and historical reality but most of all as a religious one; not as the relic of a venerable and finished past but as a reality alive through the ages. The principal features of this vitality of the Jewish people are its collective faithfulness to the One God, its fervor in studying the scriptures to discover, in the light of revelation, the meaning of human life, its search for an identity amid other men, and its constant efforts to reassemble as a new, unified community. These signs pose questions to us Christians which touch on the heart of our faith: What is the proper mission of the Jews in the divine plan? What expectations animate them, and in what respect are these expectations different from or similar to our own?

The Vatican *Guidelines* indicate the permanence of Judaism, though they do not refer to the rabbinic commentary on the biblical word, the *Mishnah* and *Midrash,* and later rabbinical literature. These commentaries represent the *halakhic* tradition central to the Jewish commitment. The *Guidelines* do, however, point out that this post-biblical tradition was "deeply affected" by the coming of Christ:

The history of Judaism did not end with the destruction of Jerusalem, but rather went on to develop a religious tradition. And, although we believe that the importance and meaning of that tradition were deeply affected by the coming of Christ, it is nonetheless rich in religious values.

The reference to the coming of Christ and what it affected requires a clarification. Does it refer to Christ as the culmination to God's promise to Abraham? If so, it is, once again, the teaching of contempt. Or is it a reference to Christian persecution of Jews? Judaism and the Jewish people were affected by laws alienating them from public life and the stream of European history. Ghettos and the wearing of humiliating badges were part of that Christian history. Is the text recognizing this reality?

THE DEICIDE ACCUSATION

The accusation of deicide has for centuries plagued the Jewish people and created a popular climate of dislike and hatred. The death of Jesus was placed on the shoulders of the Jews by church fathers and medieval theologians. Annual passion plays and pre-Vatican II catechetical teaching continued the accusation. *Nostra Aetate* refers to the matter without qualification, thereby creating a question of concern for the Jewish reader:

> True, the Jewish authorities and those who followed their lead pressed for the death of Christ; still, what happened in his passion cannot be charged against all the Jews, without distinction, then alive, nor against the Jews of today.

Some of the questions to be asked are: Who were the Jewish authorities in Roman-dominated Jerusalem? Does the text refer to the high priest, a nominee of Rome? Or does it refer to the Pharisaic scholars, the Sanhedrin leadership, or perhaps the populist leaders of the Zealot movement? It is quite difficult to determine a central Jewish authority at that time. Rabbinic literature reflects the pluralistic nature of authority by accepting several opinions on any subject discussed by the rabbis in the *Mishnah* and in the *midrashic* commentaries. Does *Nostra Aetate* include all the Jewish leadership of the time?

The reference to "Jewish authorities" pressing for Jesus' death is too vague and in part is clarified in the 1975 *Guidelines:*

> Judaism in the time of Christ and the apostles was a complex reality, embracing many different trends, many spiritual, religious, social, and cultural values.

CATHOLIC EDUCATION AND JUDAISM

Underlying *Nostra Aetate* is the requirement to present the history of Jews and Judaism in a way that reflects the gospel teaching:

> Although the Church is the new people of God, the Jews should not be presented as rejected or accursed by God, as if this followed from the Holy Scriptures. All should see to it, then, that in catechetical work or in the preaching of the word of God, they do not teach anything that does not conform to the truth of the Gospel and the spirit of Christ.

These recommendations have been followed in the United States by the Department of Education of the United States Catholic Conference. Together with the Anti-Defamation League of B'nai B'rith, special courses on Jews and Judaism for Catholic teachers were developed. The educational program, *Understanding the Jewish Experience,* offers background information on Judaism from the earliest days to the twentieth century's experience, in the fields of theology, liturgy and history. *Abraham, Our Father in Faith,* edited by the Superintendent of Schools' Office of the Archdiocese of Philadelphia, and jointly republished by the National Conference of Catholic Bishops—Secretariat of Catholic-Jewish Relations and the Anti-Defamation League of B'nai B'rith, is part of this educational project. The booklet provides teachers on the elementary and secondary levels with background and classroom materials on Judaism that can be easily incorporated in the teaching of the Catholic religion and the presentation of Jews and Judaism.

The *Nostra Aetate* educational recommendation was expanded in the Vatican II 1985 document *Notes on the Correct Way to Present the Jews and Judaism in Preaching and Catechesis of the Roman Catholic Church.*

The new document is called by the modest title *Notes,* conveying a less formal—perhaps less finished—role than the one played by the two previous Vatican II documents. It is the product of several writers and consultants who worked on the document for three years. There is the impression that they have produced a document, but not necessarily achieved a consensus. There seem to be at least two distinct, sometimes opposing, points of view at work that would create in the Jewish reader a sense of confusion. One trend would seem to deny Judaism and the Jewish people an ongoing place in God's design. The other affirms the eternal validity of Israel's testimony. Both require a reflective observation. The *Notes* have the following positive and negative aspects seen from a Jewish point of view:

Positive Aspects

1. COVENANT.

Basing itself on the words of Pope John Paul II at Mainz (1980) the *Notes* affirm that the covenant between God and the Jewish people "has never been revoked."

2. THE JEWISH ROOTS OF CHRISTIANITY.

The *Notes* stress that "Jesus was and always remained a Jew."

3. CARE IN READING THE NEW TESTAMENT.

The *Notes* urge Catholic teachers and preachers to take special care in their reading of the New Testament:

> Hence it cannot be ruled out that some references hostile or less than favorable to the Jews, have their historical context in conflicts with the nascent Church and the Jewish community. Certain controversies reflect Christian-Jewish relations long after the time of Jesus. To establish this is of capital importance if we wish to bring out the meaning of certain Gospel texts for the Christians of today. All this should be taken into account when preparing catechesis and homilies for the last week of Lent and Holy Week.

4. THE PHARISEES.

The *Notes* make the educator aware of the close relationship of Jesus to the Pharisaic movement.

— It is Pharisees who warn Jesus of the risks he is running (Lk 13:31).
— Some Pharisees are praised—e.g., "the scribe" of Mark 12:34.
— Jesus eats with Pharisees (Lk 7:36, 14:1).
— Jesus shares, with the majority of Palestinians Jews of that time, certain pharisaic doctrines—the concept of the resurrection of the body; forms of piety such as almsgiving, prayer, fasting (cf. Mt 6:1–18), and the liturgical practice of addressing God as father; the priority of the commandment to love God and one's neighbor (cf. Mk 12:28–34). This also applies to Paul (cf. Acts 23:8), who

always considered his membership among the Pharisees as a title of honor (cf. ibid 23:6, 26:5; Phil 3:5).

The *Notes* remind the catechists that "the Pharisees are not mentioned in the accounts of the Passion."

5. CONDEMNATION OF ANTI-SEMITISM.

The *Notes* echo *Nostra Aetate* and the *Guidelines* in the condemnation of anti-Semitism.

6. HOLOCAUST AND THE STATE OF ISRAEL.

The *Notes* state that "catechesis should help in understanding the meaning for the Jews of the extermination during the years 1939–1945, and its consequences." The Holocaust, however, should be understood by humanity, especially all who profess faith in a living God. The Holocaust occurred in Christian Europe, in the midst of Western Christian civilization, in an almost complete silence from Christians and Christian religious organizations.

Two paragraphs refer to Israel, the land and the state. To our knowledge, it is the first time that the Vatican has referred to the State of Israel in an official document. The text on the land is taken from the U.S. National Conference of Catholic Bishops' document on Catholic-Jewish dialogue, pointing out the unbroken attachment of Jews to the Promised Land.

The reference to the State of Israel suggests that educators should understand Israel in political terms only, "in reference to the common principles of international law." This suggestion disregards the millennia of the Jewish relationship to the land of Israel and Jerusalem, and the proclamation of this relationship in the daily liturgy, in the Passover celebration, and in almost all areas of Jewish spirituality. While the Jewish reader is concerned with the exclusion of the theological dimensions of the State of Israel, he is hopeful that the reference to international law is indicative of a new development: an anticipation of the formal exchange of ambassadors between the Vatican and the State of Israel.

Negative Aspects

Aware as we are that the *Notes* represent "a text of the Catholic Church" (cf. Monsignor Jorge Mejia, Vatican press conference, June

24th) we are concerned about certain sections of the document. It is our responsibility as partners in dialogue to point out, frankly and without cavil, that which is negative and even detrimental to Judaism. Our concern is that the consequences of reinforcing certain negative teachings can, as in the past, directly affect relations between Catholics and Jews.

The following points require further examination or a joint Catholic-Jewish reflection:

1. ELECTION.

The *Notes* seem to deny Jews their own validity, their place in God's design:

> Thus the definitive meaning of the election of Israel does not become clear except in the light of a complete fulfillment (Romans 9–11) and an election in Jesus Christ. . . .

2. SALVATION AND TRIUMPHALISM.

The *Notes* state that

> "In virtue of her divine mission, the Church," which is to be the "all-embracing means of salvation" in which alone "the fullness of the means of salvation can be obtained" (*Unitatis Redintegratio,* 3) "must of her nature proclaim Jesus Christ to the world." Jesus affirms (John 10:16 cf. *Guidelines and Suggestions* I) that "there shall be one flock and one shepherd." Church and Judaism cannot then be seen as two parallel ways of salvation and the Church must witness to Christ as the redeemer for all, while "maintaining the strictest respect for religious liberty in line with the teaching of the Second Vatican Council (*Dignitatis Humanae*) (*Guidelines and Suggestions,* I).

While we recognize the right and mission of each religion to proclaim its faith commitment and spirituality, we cannot accept the notion of exclusivity: the denial of the other's vocation as a way of God. The *Notes'* remarks remind one of the statements of Cyprian and Origen: *Extra Ecclesiam Nulla Salus*—"outside the Church there is no salvation." This is the theological thinking that, for centuries, nurtured Christian teaching of contempt causing untold degradation and pain to Jews in Europe. It makes difficult, almost impossible, a respectful relationship which is aware of differences yet conscious of being partners in God's design.

3. TYPOLOGY.

Typology is recommended as the method to read the Hebrew Bible. The typological reading interprets, as the *Notes* do, central biblical events as pre-intuitions of Christianity. It defines the Exodus as "an experience of salvation and liberation that is not complete in itself." A reading of the Book of Exodus shows that the completion of the political liberation from Egyptian slavery is God's revelation at Sinai, the giving of the commandments and the ethical summons that sealed the Covenant with God. Sinai was the ultimate expression of liberation, a spiritual liberation ignored by the *Notes*. It is surprising that the Vatican *Notes* and liberation theologians seem to agree on their typological reading of the Exodus event. The liberation theologians add to it their own ideological emphasis. But for both the Exodus of the Jews is a typological reference preparing the way for Jesus' liberation. The Book of Exodus is read up to Chapter 19. The rest, commandments and daily ritual, chapters 20 to 40, are totally disregarded.

4. JESUS' DEATH.

The *Notes* deal with the serious and far-reaching accusation which Christians have made against the Jews from time immemorial right up to the present. It is the accusation that the Jews crucified Jesus. In section 4, number 22, the *Notes* record the trial and death of Jesus. It places the blame on the "authorities of the Jews and those who followed their lead for the death of Christ," in accord with the *Nostra Aetate* statement. As was said before, it is very difficult to identify "Jewish authorities" under Roman rule. Why repeat this concept that has no concrete historical basis? The *Notes,* following Vatican II, stress that "Christ in his boundless love freely underwent his passion and death because of the sins of all men, so that all might attain salvation." If this is so, why blame the so-called Jewish authorities and continue a tradition that accuses Jews of deicide?

5. RELATIONSHIP OF THE HEBREW BIBLE TO THE NEW TESTAMENT.

The *Notes* state:

> The singular character and the difficulty of Christian teaching about Jews and Judaism lies in this, that it needs to balance a number of pairs of ideas which express the relation between the two economies of the Old and New Testaments:—promise and fulfillment;—continuity and newness;—singularity and universality; [etc.].

How are these opposites to be "balanced" by Catholic educators? The *Notes* give no indication of how this can be achieved. On the contrary, here the reader can see only the theology of dispensationalism: Christianity fulfilling in the New Testament that which was promised in the Hebrew Bible.

THE NOTES' CONTRIBUTION

The *Notes* resonate from a Jewish understanding with both positive and negative dimensions. They also resonate with apparent contradictions. It is well that the *Notes* accord to Jews and Judaism—historically and currently—a fuller recognition of Israel's being and mission. In addition, the *Notes* go further than any prior Catholic document in pointing to Jesus' Jewishness and his close relationship to Pharisaism. Finally, the *Notes* once again condemn anti-Semitism.

Yet, on the other hand, the *Notes* echo several elements of the teaching of contempt: positing merely preparatory roles for Jews and Judaism in God's plan; continuing advice to read the Hebrew Bible through typological-Christian lenses; denial of Judaism as a way of salvation; and repeating the spurious charge of guilt in Jesus' death against unnamed and unknowable "Jewish authorities."

WITHIN CONTEXT

The Vatican *Notes* were adapted to the American Christian educational experience in 1988:

Within Context: Guidelines for the Catechetical Presentation of Jews and Judaism in the New Testament. It was prepared in cooperation with the Secretariat for Catholic-Jewish Relations of the National Conference of Catholic Bishops; the Education Department of the United States Catholic Conference; and the Anti-Defamation League of B'nai B'rith. It has been well received by Catholic educators in Europe and Latin America. There already are two French editions. German, Italian and Polish versions are to be published and a Spanish translation is underway in Montevideo, Uruguay.

Within Context is the product of a working group of twelve Catholic educators, New Testament scholars, rabbinic scholars, and publishers who met in January 1986, at Graymoor Ecumenical Institute in Garrison, New York. The Catholic participants who prepared the manuscript represented different areas of concern in the church—New Testament studies, education in general and interfaith relations.

The educational guidelines are divided into three sections covering specific areas for the information of New Testament teachers. Sections are devoted to the Jewishness of Jesus, Jewish society in Jesus' time and the Jewish roots to Christian teaching and worship.

Up to now the prevailing tendency in Christian education has been to deny any Jewish spiritual creativity at the time of Jesus. Jesus appears as the innovator and the only source of devotion and spiritual richness.

Within Context, however, points out the tremendous spiritual richness of Jewish thinking and religious life of the time: the Pharisees and their contributions, the Sadducees and the temple structure. It also contains a short essay on the Jewish roots of Christian worship. Other sections stress the need to understand Torah and gospel, the meaning of love in Judaism and Christianity and, finally, a consideration of *Halakah,* Jewish religious law.

Special attention is given to the question of Jesus' death and its presentation in passion plays. The authors of *Within Context* point out the need to understand the death of Jesus in its historical perspective, stressing that "it is crucial for catechesis to provide a proper context for understanding the death of Jesus."

They go on: "Like the New Testament as a whole, the Passion narratives of the four Gospels are not entirely eyewitness accounts of the historical event but later, post-Resurrection accounts from different perspectives on the meaning of Jesus' death and Resurrection." The authors stress that "any explanation which directly or implicitly imputes collective responsibility of the Jewish people for Jesus' death not only obscures this simple truth, but also leads to anti-Semitism." This is a crucial teaching that will change the presentation of Jews in the story of Jesus' death and avoid the old accusation of deicide with its charge of anti-Semitism.

It is my conviction that the use of the general term "the Jews" in some New Testament texts, especially in the passion narrative of the Gospel of John, can lead to an imputation of collective guilt. Thus, commendably, *Within Context* remarks that "such scenes, transmitted uncritically in the classroom, can lead to misunderstanding of the nature of the New Testament narrative and even to anti-Jewish hostility among students as history has shown all too well. Therefore, a careful attempt to contextualize the passage describing conflict between Jews and various Jewish groups is essential in catechesis today."

Within Context is indeed revolutionary! Teachers and publishers are encouraged to augment their textbooks and their teaching with materials drawn from the rich spiritual heritage of Judaism. These guidelines stress that "reclaiming the Jewish origins of Christianity, together with a sense of the continuing fruitfulness of the Church's spiritual links with the Jewish people today, can greatly enrich and deepen Christian education."

Dialogue involves mutual acceptance of the participants as equals, a mutual acceptance of the other as a being of God. It requires the acknowledgment of different faith vocations which, in turn, demands an honest and committed examination of our own theology vis-a-vis that of the other. Otherwise, as occurs in sections of the *Notes,* we are faced with what Hans Joachim Schoeps expressed in 1961:

> Even from the point of view of religious phenomenology, faith is to be had by genuine acknowledgment. As long as this view is not really accepted by Christians, there can be scarcely anything more depressing for a Jew than what the Church says about Israel, today as always, without knowledge of Israel's understanding of itself.[15]

This difficulty requires joint theological reflection in meaningful dialogue.

NOSTRA AETATE AND ANTI-SEMITISM

The Vatican Council's concern with the historical reality of anti-Semitism became evident in the general discussions and the preparation of *Nostra Aetate.* The first draft had a line "condemning" anti-Semitism. Some council fathers considered that the word "condemn" should only be employed by a Vatican Council in problems relating to dogma. Cardinal Bea, however, reminded the council of the March 25, 1928, declaration by the Vatican Congregation of the Holy Office that specifically used "condemnation" in relation to the Catholic Church's position on anti-Semitism.[16]

Nostra Aetate points out:

> Furthermore, in her rejection of every persecution against any man, the Church, mindful of her patrimony she shares with the Jews and moved not by political reasons but by the Gospel's spiritual love, decries hatred, persecutions, and displays of anti-Semitism, directed against Jews at any time and by anyone.

The Vatican *Guidelines,* ten years later, state clearly and strongly:

> Moreover, the step taken by the Council finds its historical setting in circumstances deeply affected by the memory of the persecution and massacre of Jews which took place in Europe before and during the Second World War. . . . While referring the reader back to this document (*Nostra Aetate*), we may simply restate here that the spiritual bonds and historical links binding the Church to Judaism condemn as opposed to the very spirit of Christianity all forms of anti-Semitism and discrimination which in any case the dignity of the human person alone would suffice to condemn.

The Vatican *Guidelines* manifest an understanding and consideration not yet present in *Nostra Aetate.* Both documents fail, though, to recount the past with centuries of theological contempt, that taught generations of Christians to mistrust and hate the Jewish people, if not Judaism. A searching of the heart, a genuine act of reconciliation, requires the recognition of past mistakes and the expression of hope for spiritual renewal.

A similar phenomenon is obvious in the so-called Puebla Document of the third meeting of CELAM, the Latin American Bishops' Conference of February, 1979, in Mexico. A draft of the document spoke of condemnation of anti-Semitism, but later versions, under the influence of certain groups, omitted that expression. The final version refers only to the Vatican II document on the subject. It is a serious omission considering the reality of anti-Semitism in certain Latin American countries and the constant danger of racism in those societies. Documents of bishops' conferences in the United States and Europe, however, follow the Vatican *Guidelines'* terminology and "condemn" the scourge of anti-Semitism.[17]

THE MEANING OF DIALOGUE

Nostra Aetate does not consider the nature and aims of the dialogue relationship, nor the meaning of the Catholic-Jewish dialogue. At the very beginning of the *Nostra Aetate* declaration Pope Paul VI states:

> In our time, when day by day mankind is being drawn ever closer together and ties are becoming stronger between different peoples, the Church is paying closer attention to the relationship with non-Christian religions. In her stands of fostering unity and love among men,

indeed among peoples, she considers above all what men have in common and what draws them to fellowship.

The Vatican *Guidelines* of January, 1975, after ten years of continuous joint programming and theological reflections, devote the first section of the document to a definition of dialogue:

> To tell the truth, such relations as there have been between Jew and Christian have scarcely ever risen above the level of monologue. From now on, real dialogue must be established.

> Dialogue presupposes that each side wishes to know the other, and wishes to increase and deepen its knowledge of the other. It constitutes a particularly suitable means of favoring a better mutual knowledge and, especially in the case of dialogue between Jews and Christians, of probing the riches of one's own tradition. Dialogue demands respect for the other as he is—above all, respect for his faith and his religious convictions.

The *Guidelines* underline the need for dialogue within the perspectives of each religious commitment, avoiding syncretism or an overly optimistic attitude, due to an excess of good will or desire to achieve a pleasant and comfortable situation. The *Guidelines* clearly states that,

> While it is true that a widespread air of suspicion, inspired by an unfortunate past, is still dominant in this particular area, Christians, for their part, will be able to see to what extent the responsibility is theirs and deduce practical conclusions for the future.

> In addition to friendly talks, competent people will be encouraged to meet and to study together the many problems deriving from the fundamental convictions of Judaism and of Christianity. In order not to hurt (even involuntarily) those taking part, it will be vital to guarantee, not only tact, but a great openness of spirit and diffidence with respect to one's own prejudices.

The Vatican *Guidelines* points out the need to know the other as a person of God, in his or her own commitment.

> Further still, these links and relationships render obligatory a better mutual understanding and renewed mutual esteem. On the practical level in particular, Christians must therefore strive to acquire a better

knowledge of the basic components of the religious tradition of Judaism; they must strive to learn by what essential traits the Jews define themselves in the light of their own religious experience.

ZIONISM AND ANTI-ZIONISM

There is one aspect that both *Nostra Aetate* and the Vatican *Guidelines* do not consider in their striving "to learn by what essential traits the Jews define themselves in the light of their own religious experience." One central trait is Zionism, an essential part of the Jewish vocation since biblical days (Gen 12 and other texts). The exile and the return experience of Ezra and Nehemiah, as well as the liturgical hope expressed in daily prayer and sustained in the High Holydays and Passover celebrations, symbolize the Jewish people's relationship to the Promised Land. The experience of near destruction under Nazi slavery and other forms of totalitarian persecution, and the creation of the State of Israel are central elements of contemporary Jewish identity. Those events must be taken into consideration in any attempt to understand the Jewish people and twentieth-century Judaism. Failure to do so is a serious flaw of both Vatican documents.

The documents of the American and French bishops, however, pay special attention to the centrality of the State of Israel in the existence of the Jewish people. The American document of November 1975 points out:

> In dialogue with Christians, Jews have explained that they do not consider themselves as a church, a sect, or a denomination, as is the case among Christian communities, but rather as a peoplehood that is not solely racial, ethnic or religious, but in a sense a composite of all these. It is for such reasons that an overwhelming majority of Jews see themselves bound in one way or another to the land of Israel. Most Jews see this tie to the land as essential to their Jewishness. Whatever difficulties Christians may experience in sharing this view, they should strive to understand this link between land and people which Jews have expressed in their writings and worship throughout two millennia as a longing for the homeland, holy Zion. Appreciation of this link is not to give assent to any particular religious interpretation of this bond. Nor is this affirmation meant to deny the legitimate rights of other parties in the region, or to adopt any political stance in the controversies over the Middle East, which lies beyond the purview of this statement.

The document of the French bishops takes a broader dimension discussing theological and political implications;

> The dispersion of the Jewish people should be understood in the light of its history. Though Jewish tradition considers the trials and exile of the people as a punishment for infidelities (Jeremiah 13:17; 20:21-23), it is nonetheless true that, since the time when Jeremiah addressed his letter to the exiles in Babylon (29:1-23), the life of the Jewish people in the diaspora has also held a positive meaning. Throughout its trials, the Jewish people has been called to "sanctify the name" amid the nations of the world. Christians must constantly combat the anti-Jewish and Manichean temptations to regard the Jewish people as accursed, under the pretext of its constant persecutions. According to the testimony of Scripture (Isaiah 53:2-2), being subjected to persecution is often an effect and reminder of the prophetic vocation.

> Today more than ever, it is difficult to pronounce a well-considered theological opinion on the return of the Jewish people to "its" land. In this context, we Christians must first of all not forget the gift, once made by God to the people of Israel, of a land where it was called to be reunited (cf. Genesis 12:7; 26:3-4, 28:13, Isaiah 43:5-7; Jeremiah 16:15; Sophronias 3:20).

> Throughout history, Jewish existence has always been divided between life among the nations and the wish for national existence on that land. This aspiration poses numerous problems even to Jews. To understand it, as well as all dimensions of the resulting discussion, Christians must not be carried away by interpretations that would ignore the forms of Jewish communal and religious life, or by political positions that, though generous, are nonetheless hastily arrived at. Christians must take into account the interpretation given by Jews to their ingathering around Jerusalem which, according to their faith, is considered a blessing. Justice is put to the test by this return and its repercussions. On the political level, it has caused confrontations between various claims for justice. Beyond the legitimate divergence of political options, the conscience of the world community cannot refuse the Jewish people, who had to submit to so many vicissitudes in the course of its history, the right and means for a political existence among the nations. At the same time, this right and the opportunities for existence cannot be refused to those who, in the course of local conflicts resulting from this return, are now victims of grave injustice.

> Let us, then, turn our eyes toward this land visited by God and let us actively hope that it may become a place where one day all its inhabitants, Jews and non-Jews, can live together in peace. It is an

essential question, faced by Christians as well as Jews, whether or not the ingathering of the dispersed Jewish people—which took place under pressure of persecution and by the play of political forces—will despite so many tragic events prove to be one of the final ways of God's justice for Jewish people and at the same time for all the nations of the earth. How could Christians remain indifferent to what is now being decided in that land?

THE EVER-PRESENT SCOURGE OF ANTI-SEMITISM

Deeply concerned with the dangers and iniquities of racism and anti-Semitism, the Holy See's Pontifical Commission, "Justice and Peace," on February 10, 1989, issued a document *The Church and Racism: Towards a More Fraternal Society.* In an honest way, the document denounces racism and at the same time confesses religious involvement in past racist attitudes:

> Of course, Christians themselves must humbly admit that members of the Church, on all levels, have not always lived out this teaching [the Christian teaching denouncing racism] coherently throughout history. Nonetheless, she must continue to proclaim what is right while seeking to do "the truth."

The Church and Racism deals with many problems of the past: racism in Antiquity; Greek and Roman attitudes toward other people; the attitude of the Church vis-a-vis the Indians in America; medieval anti-Judaism. The document describes past mistakes with a sincerity that touches the heart of the reader and invites Catholics, as well as other faith communities, to ponder the meaning of racism in history.

The Church and Racism complements the thinking of previous Vatican documents on anti-Semitism. It points out the roots of Nazi anti-Semitism, stating that 18th-century racism, using "science" to justify prejudice, "had considerable resonance in Germany" and influenced the Nazi decisions that produced one of the greatest "genocides in history":

> This murderous folly struck first and foremost the Jewish people in unheard-of proportions, as well as other people, such as Gypsies and the Tziganes and also categories of persons such as the handicapped and the mentally ill. It was only a step from racism to eugenics, and it was quickly taken.

It is true that the Nazis included in their racist program the destruction of Poles and Russians, Gypsies and handicapped people, but the Jewish case was unique. Jews were sentenced to death by reason of birth; the Nuremberg laws were part of a state ideology of immolation. This is recognized by the document when it refers specifically to the *Shoah* as the "Jewish Holocaust."

The Vatican document devotes Section 15 to denounce anti-Semitism and anti-Zionism:

> Among the manifestations of systematic racial distress, specific mention must once again be made of anti-Semitism. If anti-Semitism has been the most tragic form that racist ideology has assumed in our century, with the horrors of the Jewish Holocaust, it has unfortunately not yet entirely disappeared. As if some had nothing to learn from the crimes of the past, certain organizations with branches in many countries keep alive an anti-Semite racist myth, with the support of networks of publications.
>
> Terrorist acts which have Jewish persons or symbols as their targets have multiplied in recent years and showed the radicalism of such groups. Anti-Zionism—which is not of the same order, since it questions the State of Israel and its policies—serves at times as a screen for anti-Semitism, feeding on it and leading to it. Furthermore, some countries impose undue harrassment and restrictions on the free emigration of Jews.

The Vatican document *The Church and Racism* rebukes the U.N. 1975 resolution calling Zionism a form of racism. The U.N. statement was described by the American bishops as "unjust." The President of the U.S. Bishops Conference stated that "its substantial inadequacy both retards the necessary struggle against racism in the world and opens the door to harrassment, discrimination and denial of basic rights to members of the Jewish community throughout the world." The Vatican criticism reinforces this condemnation.

TOWARD A JEWISH UNDERSTANDING OF CHRISTIANITY

Jewish theological considerations of Christianity are not normative statements of the synagogue. They are individual responses based in Jewish tradition. The community might or might not accept these proposals. The individual Jew, member of the community, represents his/her search and commitment. The attempt to understand Christianity is not an invitation to conversion or syncretism, but to understand and recognize Christianity as the other, in faith, as a person of God. Christianity and Judaism in the present reality of dialogue and encounter require mutual understanding and recognition.

Understanding and recognition entail a concept of community. It is a community of faith coming to God through different calls. It follows the definition stated by Rabbi Joseph B. Soloveitchik: "A community is established the very moment I recognize the thou and extend greetings to the thou. One individual extends the 'shalom' greeting to another individual; and in so doing he creates a community—recognition means sacrificial action: The individual who withdraws in order to make room for the thou."

Rabbi Soloveitchik clarifies the significance of recognition in an essential manner that defines the very value of the dialogue encounter:

Quite often a man finds himself in a crowd amongst strangers. He feels lonely. No one knows him, no one cares for him, no one is concerned with him. It is again an existential experience. He begins to doubt his ontological worth. This leads to alienation from the crowd surrounding him. Suddenly someone taps him on the shoulder and says: "Aren't you Mr. So-and-So? I have heard so much about you." In a fraction of a second his awareness changes. An alien being turns into a fellow member of an existential community (the crowd). What brought about the change? The recognition by somebody, the word!

To recognize a person is not just to identify him physically. It is more than that: It is an act of identifying him existentially, as a person who has a job to do, that only he can do properly.

To recognize a person means to affirm that he is irreplaceable. To hurt a person means to tell him that he's expendable, that there is no need for him.

Recognition implies a sense of responsibility, as Soloveitchik points out:

Once I have recognized the thou I invited him to join the community, I *ipso facto* assumed responsibility for the thou. Recognition is identical with commitment. Here again, we walk in the ways of our Maker. God created man; God did not abandon him; God showed concern for him. God cared for Adam; God said: It is not good for man to be alone. He provided him with a mate; he placed him in Paradise, and allowed him to enjoy the fruits of the Garden. Even after man sinned and was exiled from the Garden, the Almighty did not desert him. Of course, he

punished him. Yet he was concerned with man even while man was in
sin. In a word, God assumed responsibility for whatever and whoever
he created: "He gives bread to all flesh for his loving kindness is ever-
lasting" (Psalm 136:25). As we have said above, the same relationship
should prevail between me and the thou whom I have recognized, and
with whom I have formed a community. I assumed responsibility for
each member of the community to whom I have granted recognition
and whom I have found worthy of being my companion. In other
words, the I is responsible for the physical and mental welfare of the
thou.[18]

Recognition is an invitation to be part of a community of faith aware
and open to differences. Dialogue in community is to recognize the other
as a person with a meaning. Martin Buber states this as basic in the
human relationship:

Once one ceases to regard the other as merely an object of observation
and begins to regard the other as an independent other standing over
against him, then we have the beginning of the I-Thou relation.[19]

A Jewish understanding of Christianity after Auschwitz and Vatican
II, in a democratic society, and beyond disputation, is the beginning of a
process that touches deeply into our faith commitments. Understanding
presupposes the recognition of that which needs comprehension. It is a
first step: to recognize Christianity, to perceive it as a faith enacted in
history, as a ray of God conveying to humanity the Eternal's message.
Christianity is in the process of being perceived, accepted, as a manifestation of God, with a mission and a message. Jewish thinking, the Jewish
people must overcome what Christians have done to Jews through the
centuries, and seek to understand Christianity and its call to serve God.

Understanding becomes a creative reality when we realize that we
relate, that we are together. To be together does not mean to lose our
identities, our religious vocations. It does not mean any form of syncretism, which should be avoided as a dangerous, meaningless aberration.
We are together, witnessing God in our respective, unique conditions,
together and at the same time individually committed to our faiths.

Christianity and Judaism have special missions in witnessing God.
Martin Buber has rightly pointed out these unique ways:

The faith of Judaism and the faith of Christendom are by nature different in kind, each in conformity with its human basis, and they will
indeed remain different, until mankind is gathered in from the exiles of

the "religions" into a kingship of God. But in Israel's striving after the renewal of its faith through the rebirth of the person and Christianity's striving for the renewal of its faith through the rebirth of nations will have something as yet unsaid to say to each other and help to give to one another—hardly to be conceived at the present time.[20]

A FINAL REFLECTION

The Christian-Jewish relationship has undergone a particular transformation. It has gone from argument to dialogue, from conflict to a situation of meeting, from ignorance and alienation to encounter, a conversation between equals. The road has not been smooth, and problems and misunderstandings still abound. But mainly there is a desire to listen and to respond, to see the other as a person and not an object of contempt.

The dialogue requires a reckoning and a reflection. Jews must deal with two thousand years of memories, memories from the times of the New Testament experience, medieval disputations, the Inquisition, and present-day Christian ideological criticisms of Zionism and Israel. Jews have to overcome the castrating effects of images transmitted by generations, and the concrete experiences of Christian triumphalism associated with political regimes past and present. Christian self-searching as evidenced in Vatican II and other Christian efforts, are the means that will open new roads to spiritual understanding.

Dialogue is both a process of inner cleansing and a search for truth. The inner cleansing is an attempt to see the other faith commitment as part of God's special design for mankind. A respectful relationship, that at this point we call dialogue until a more precise word can describe this unique, special meeting, is never a confrontation but a common endeavor, mindful of the different vocations. Real dialogue calls persons into their own being while also acknowledging the others as persons with a way and a commitment. Religious dialogue is a recognition of the other as person, and God as the common ground of being.

The search into the meaning of God's special call is search for the meaning of our faith encounter beyond syncretism and sporadic sympathies. Ours is a search for the mystery of a new dimension: the possibility to witness God together, not unified, but standing together at a time of general unbelief and ideological triumphalism. Ours is a search in humility for God's presence and call.

The promulgation of *Nostra Aetate,* the publication of the Vatican

Guidelines, the *Notes, The Church and Racism,* and the Episcopal documents on Christian-Jewish relations are good signs, signs of peace, signs marking the beginning of a prophetic time and a prophetic relationship. Jews and Christians together have embarked on a new time, a time of hope, a time of encounter and dialogue.

NOTES

1. Martin Buber, *Die Stunde und die Erkenntnis* (Berlin: Schocken, 1936), p. 155.

2. Joseph L. Lichten, "The Council's Statement on the Jews," in *Christian Friends' Bulletin* (December 1965).

3. Charles Glock and Rodney Stark, *Christian Beliefs and Anti-Semitism* (New York: Harper & Row, 1966).

4. Quoted in Vincent A. Yzermans, *American Participation in the Second Vatican Council* (New York: Sheed & Ward, 1967), pp. 573–574.

5. Arthur Gilbert, *The Vatican Council and the Jews* (Cleveland and New York: The World Publishing Company, 1968), p. 147.

6. Ibid., p. 300.

7. Cf. Solomon Grayzel, *The Church and the Jews in the XIIIth Century* (New York: Hermon Press, 1966), pp. 76–78.

8. Joseph B. Soloveitchik, "Confrontation," in Norman Lamm and Walter S. Wurzburger, eds., *A Treasury of Tradition* (New York: Hebrew Publishing, 1967), p. 80.

9. Eliezer Berkovits, "Judaism in the Post-Christian Era," in *Judaism* (January 1966), p. 74.

10. Jacob B. Agus, *Dialogue and Tradition* (New York: Abelard-Schuman, 1971), p. 102.

11. Cf. Thomas F. Stransky, "The Guidelines, A Catholic Point of View," and Leon Klenicki, "The Guidelines, A Jewish Point of View," in *Face to Face:* An Interreligious Bulletin I (Summer 1975) 7–13.

12. All quotations from *Nostra Aetate,* the Vatican *Guidelines,* and the various bishops' conference statements are from Helga Croner, comp., *Stepping Stones to Further Jewish-Christian Relations,* (London-New York, Stimulus Books, 1977).

13. Helga Croner, comp., *More Stepping Stones To Jewish-Christian Relations.* An unabridged collection of Christian documents 1975–1983 (New York: Paulist, A Stimulus Book, 1985).

14. Cf. Walter Jacob, *Christianity Through Jewish Eyes* (Cincinnati: Hebrew Union College, 1974).

15. Cf. Hans J. Schoeps, *The Jewish-Christian Argument* (New York: Holt, Rinehart & Winston, 1963).

16. Cf. Augustin Cardinal Bea, *The Church and the Jewish People* (New York: Harper & Row, 1966).

17. Leon Klenicki, "The Presentation of Jews and Judaism in the Puebla Document, A Report" (New York: Anti-Defamation League of B'nai B'rith, 1979). Cf. also, John Eagleson and Philip Scharper, eds., *Puebla and Beyond* (Maryknoll, N.Y.: Orbis Press, 1979), pp. 250–262.

18. Joseph B. Soloveitchik, "The Community", (*Tradition,* New York, Vol. 17, No. 2, Spring 1978).

19. Martin Buber, *Two Types of Faith,* (New York, Harper Torch Books, 1951).

20. Ibid, pp. 173–174.

V.
A NEW MATURITY IN
CHRISTIAN-JEWISH DIALOGUE

A New Maturity in Christian-Jewish Dialogue: An Annotated Bibliography 1975–1989

Eugene J. Fisher

In an article in *Judaism* (Winter, 1982), Professor Michael Wyschogrod concludes a review-essay of two Catholic attempts to reformulate traditional Christian understandings of the relationship between the church and the Jewish people with the comment that, today, "A new stage has been reached in the dialogue between Judaism and Christianity." He goes on to caution that the authors represent "the frontiers of Christian thought" on the topic, leaving the impression that the two authors, both eminent European scholars, are somewhat isolated within the Christian community in general, and the Catholic community in particular.

This assessment is both true and not true. It is true that the works cited, those of Fathers Clemens Thoma and Franz Mussner (see below), are on the "frontiers" of contemporary Christian scholarship, and that the vast majority of Christians are not yet familiar with their works and thought. Much work remains to be done to translate the efforts of the scholars to the level of the pulpit and classrooms that provide the church's "delivery system" in implementing the transformation of Christian attitudes toward Jews mandated by the Second Vatican Council, and explicated with increasing forcefulness in subsequent official statements by Protestant and Catholic church bodies alike.

But it is not true to imply that the task that scholars such as Mussner and Thoma have set for themselves, the turning around (*teshuvah* is an apt term for it) of the church's centuries-long "teaching of contempt" against Jews and Judaism is an isolated effort. In two previous annotated bibliographies (*Origins*, National Catholic News Service, Vol. 7, 1977, pp. 207–09; and Vol. 8, 1978, pp. 284–86), I have attempted to keep track of the virtual explosion of works on both the scholarly and popular level which have been produced in the last decade. This paper updates these reports for the years 1979 through 1989, and incorporates works of more lasting interest first included there. For earlier works (up to 1975), see *The Study of Judaism: Bibliographic Essays* (Vols. I and II, Bibliographic Essays in Medieval Jewish Studies, Anti-Defamation League, 1972, 1976.)

In his brilliant study paper on "The Mission and Witness of the Church" in the light of the dialogue, presented to the International Vatican-Jewish Liaison Committee in Venice in 1977, and published in *Fifteen Years of Catholic-Jewish Dialogue 1970–1985* (Rome: Libreria Editrice Lateranense, 1988), Professor Tommaso Federici of the Pontifical Urbaniana University noted that the Conciliar declaration itself rode on the crest of a wave of biblical, liturgical, systematic and ecclesiological thinking that set its brief paragraphs into a much broader movement of Christian renewal and reformation. From the point of view of official statements alone, Federici was able to claim with justifiable confidence that the movement was "irreversible." Whatever may happen (though there is no reason for complacency when confronting the hydra-headed monster of anti-Semitism), there is absolutely no chance that the church in our time will step back into the simplistic triumphalism of the past.

This chapter seeks to chronicle only the last few years' worth of the explosion of new literature that has so irrevocably changed for the better our perceptions of each other as religious communities. One change to note within the dialogue in what follows, is the willingness of Christian and Jewish thinkers alike to take up with new candor even the most sensitive of issues, both contemporary and traditional, which can divide as well as unite us. This willingness, while opening up certain difficulties, indicates, I believe, a maturity in the dialogue that would have been inconceivable even to many of the pioneers among us who marked the paths we follow today. Yet it is our ability to handle the divisive issues, as well as to explore our commonalities, that in the long run will test the viability of our dialogue.

1. DOCUMENTING THE DIALOGUE

Stepping Stones to Further Jewish-Christian Relations, edited by Helga Croner (London, New York: Stimulus, 1977) is an indispensable tool. It contains the text of virtually every major document, Catholic or Protestant, international (Vatican, World Council of Churches) or local (U. S., Europe, Latin America) that was issued by a major Christian denomination since the late 1940s. Croner has updated her collection in *More Stepping Stones* (New York: Paulist, 1985, $7.95).

For maintaining an ongoing file of church documents, I would recommend subscribing to SIDIC (via del Plebiscito 112, Rome 00186, Italy), a journal sponsored by the Sisters of Zion in Rome. It is entirely devoted to Jewish-Christian relations and regularly publishes and interprets major statements, such as the 1980 statement of the Protestant (Evangelical) Synod of the Rhineland; Cardinal Etchegaray's poignant intervention at the 1983 Synod of Catholic Bishops in Rome, which called for reconciliation with the Jews on the deepest religious grounds; and the more recent document of the Holy See's Council, "Iustitia et Pax," on *The Church and Racism,* which interprets the history of Anti-Semitism.

Christology After Auschwitz, by Michael B. McGarry, C.S.P. (N.Y.: Paulist, 1977) provides an excellent companion piece to the documents. Centering on a single core issue, this reworked thesis, originally done for the University of Toronto, offers a concise analysis and overview of the positions taken in the statements included in *Stepping Stones.* Though at times a little too neat in his categories, the author provides in this short book (107 pages) an excellent summary of the state of the question on such matters as the current attempt to work out a Christian eschatology that would not be dependent upon the ancient idea that Judaism's role in the history of salvation was abrogated by the coming of Christ. Michael Shermis' *Jewish-Christian Relations: An Annotated Bibliography and Resource Guide* (Indiana University Press, 1988) includes not only books, organized into nineteen categories, but surveys of articles, journals, media and organizations working in the field. It is a very handy reference tool for the practitioner of dialogue.

The International Jewish Committee for Interreligious Consultation (IJCIC) regularly engages in high-level meetings with Roman Catholic and major international Protestant bodies. Its papers exchanged with the International Catholic-Jewish Liaison Committee, from 1970–1985 are included in the above-mentioned *Fifteen Years,* along with key statements of the pope and the Vatican Commission for Religious Relations with the Jews. In the last few years meetings with the World Anglican Communion, the World Lutheran Federation (LWF), and Orthodox bodies have joined the more established international Vatican-Jewish Liaison Committee and IJCIC's ongoing dialogue with the World Council of Churches. The papers from these dialogues are normally made available in English in journals such as SIDIC, the *Journal of Ecumenical Studies* (Temple University), and *Christian-Jewish Relations: A Documentary Survey* (11 Hertford Street, London W1Y 7DX, Great Britain). Topics taken up in the agendas of these meetings, such as "Martin Luther and the Jews" in the IJCIC/WLF dialogue, and "The Sanctity of Life in An Age of Violence" in the Vatican-IJCIC Consultation, illustrate the above-mentioned willingness to tackle the tough questions of both history and contemporary society. *Immanuel,* the journal of the Ecumenical Theological Research Fraternity in Israel (P.O.B. 249, Jerusalem) is an excellent source for scholarly articles reflecting the dialogue in Israel.

Recent statements of official church bodies reflect the increasing effectiveness and depth of the formal dialogues and parallel scholarly work. The remarkable series of papal pronouncements culminating in the critically important address of the pope to the Jewish community of Mainz in Germany in November of 1980, and at the Synagogue in Rome in 1986, for example, can be found in E. Fisher and L. Klenicki, eds., *John Paul II on Jews and Judaism* (U. S. Catholic Conference, Washington, D. C., 1987), published in Spanish by Ediciones Paulinas (Buenos Aires, 1988). For those who read French, M.T. Hoch and B. Dupuy have edited *Les Eglises devant le Judaïsme, Documents Officiels 1948–1978* (Paris: Cerf, 1980) which parallels and to some extent updates the entries in Croner's original *Stepping Stones. John Paul II on the Holocaust* (USCC, 1988), edited by Eugene Fisher, includes papal texts on the Shoah through 1988.

In this country, one of the most significant dialogues being held began in 1979 between representatives of the Synagogue Council of America and the Catholic Bishops' Conference. The papers from the first round, which focused reflectively on issues such as family policy, national economic policy and international human rights, have been edited by Eugene Fisher and Daniel Polish in *The Formation of Social Policy in the Catholic and Jewish Traditions* (University of Notre Dame Press, 1980). The second volume of papers, also edited by Fisher and Polish, *Liturgical Foundations of Social Policy in the Catholic and Jewish Traditions* (University of Notre Dame Press, 1983) probes the way in which Christian and Jewish styles of worship influence their respective social visions in terms of such contemporary issues as health care and healing, the quest for justice and peace, and conservation ethics. Liturgist Lawrence Hoffman's introductory and concluding "Assessment" Essays neatly encapsulate the volume.

The dialogue in this country is unique both in its diversity and in the major contributions arising from local levels. A prime example of the latter can be found in the joint Catholic-Jewish statements of two Los Angeles groups begun in the 1970s by the Los Angeles Archdiocese and the local Board of Rabbis. Their "Priest/Rabbi" group has produced model statements in dialogue format on "Covenant or Covenants?" (March, 1979) and "Kingdom of God" (Summer, 1982). The Respect Life Committee has issued provocative joint statements on abortion (1977), care for the dying (1979), and nuclear armaments (1982). All of the statements, through 1987, have been collected and published in loose-leaf binder form (Archdiocese of Los Angeles, 1988), forming together an invaluable record of and model for local dialogues.

Protestant-Jewish dialogues have also been highly productive. *Evangelicals and Jews in Conversation* (Grand Rapids: Baker, 1978), edited jointly by Dr. Marvin Wilson of Gordon College, and Rabbis Marc Tanenbaum and James Rudin of the American Jewish Committee, presents a glimpse into the beginnings of a new area of Jewish-Christian relations in this country. An interdenominational group of conservative Christian scholars share views with their Jewish counterparts on issues of scripture, theology, history and social ethics. This is a highly important documentation of a dialogue in progress.

Tanenbaum, Wilson and Rudin have combined again to edit the second volume of papers documenting the Evangelical/Jewish dialogue: *Evangelicals and Jews in An Age of Pluralism* (Grand Rapids: Baker Book House, 1984). The fifteen essays by leading Evangelical and Jewish scholars illustrate the increasing willingness of the two communities to tackle the more delicate social and theological questions, such as the nature of biblical interpretation, atonement and redemption, mission and proselytism, and the Holocaust. The candor and cross-referencing of each other's materials show the deepening awareness of the "other" that flows from true dialogue. A third volume of essays from this ongoing dialogue is now being prepared. Written for Evangelicals, but also of interest to all Christians, is Wilson's ambitious *Our Father Abraham,* which ranges through biblical, theological and historical questions with a sure step and steady judgment.

Another collection of dialogues can be found in *Speaking of God Today: Jews and Lutherans in Conversation,* edited by Paul Ophals and Marc Tanenbaum (Philadelphia: Fortress, 1974). Topics include such trichotomies as "Law-Grace-Election" and "Land-People-State." Tanenbaum has also combined with Orthodox scholar N. Vaporis to edit the papers of a major "Greek Orthodox-Jewish Consultation" (Special issue, *The Greek Orthodox Theological Review,* Vol. 22:1, Spring 1977: cf. the Fall, 1976, issue of the *Journal of Ecumenical Studies*).

More recently, Eugene Fisher has collaborated with Rabbis Tanenbaum and Rudin to co-edit *Twenty Years of Jewish-Catholic Relations* (New York: Paulist, 1986), which includes assessments of developments in biblical, liturgical, educational and theological understandings since the Second Vatican Council, as well as retrospectives on the council itself.

On the international level there exists a richness of consultations, many resulting in significant collections of papers. The report on the World Council of Churches' Consultation on the Church and the Jewish People which met in Jerusalem in June of 1977, for example, was edited by Franz van Hammerstein under the title, *Christian-Jewish Relations in Ecumenical Perspective* (Geneva: World Council of Churches, 1978). The volume features a keynote lecture by Krister Stendahl attempting to place Jewish-Christian Relations "In the Wider Perspective of Dialogue with People of Other Faiths and Ideologies." The unique thrust of the bulk of the volume, however, is indicated by its subtitle: "with special emphasis on Africa." Contributions from African scholars representing seven countries dealing with a range of issues from the theological (e.g., "The Concept of God in Jewish and African Traditions," J. Mbiti of Kenya) to the sociocultural (e.g., "Sacrifice" by D. Mondeh and "Rites of Passage" by F. Abotchie, both of Ghana). For those interested in the dialogue as perceived in Africa there is a special issue of SIDIC on "Africa and Judaism" (Vol. 11, No. 2, 1978). Articles and documents concerning the international dialogue are regularly featured in *Current Dialogue,* issued by the "People of Living Faiths" section of the World Council of Churches (150 route de Ferney, P.O. Box 66, 1211 Geneva 20, Switzerland).

Also organized as a consultation rather than a dialogue as such (i.e., where Jewish and Christian scholars each address the same topics) are the papers from the 1982 Lutheran World Federation's "Fourth International Consultation" on "The Significance of Judaism for the Life and Mission of the Church," published in *LWF Studies* (Geneva: LWF Department of Studies, 1983). Here are gathered some excellent papers on both "sides" of the dialogue, such as those on "Torah" and "The Election and Vocation of Israel" by the Jewish "consultants" Jean Halperin and Uriel Simon, and that by Seminex scholar Ralph W. Klein on "The Origin and Nature of Our Estrangement." I must say, however, that I found disquieting some of the "theses" presented by LWF staff secretary and conference organizer, Arne Sovik, who rather quickly dismisses a core biblical theme (as well as the "special status . . . of the Old Testament as scripture") by stating blandly (Thesis V, 3) that: "Dealing with Israel as a 'chosen people' is not ethically possible for Christians" (p. 59). This is a reductionist universalism which, of course, opens the way for the quite logical conclusion that the New Testament itself should have no "special status," and that Jesus as the Christ is not unique, since Sovik's "ethical" critique is as easily applicable to these fundamental Christian claims as it is to the Hebrew scriptures. Even the shared assertion of the oneness and uniqueness of God would logically fall to this sort of critique. Without "particularity" (i.e., historical acknowledgment), it can be asserted, there simply is no such thing as religion or faith. There remains only philosophy.

On a less official level, two other works illustrating the range of international dialogue can be included here. First, there is *Christianity in the Holy Land: Papers Read at the 1979 Tantur Conference,* edited by Catholic Israeli scholar D.-M.A. Jaeger for Theological Research (Jerusalem: Franciscan Printing Press, 1981). The papers, given by Protestant, Catholic and Orthodox scholars all living in Jerusalem at the time and reproduced in their original languages (mainly English, but also French and German) cover the agenda of the dialogue from the history of the relationship to theology (see especially those of L. Volken, J. Schoneveld, and M.J. Dubois), spirituality ("Monasticism in the Holy Land" by Y. de Broucker), Ecumenism (F. Bouwen, W. H. Brown), Hebrew Christianity (O.C.M. Kvarme) and Arab Christianity (S. Khalil). This last essay, at some 100 tight pages, is a small book in itself (in French). Surveying the theological dialogue in Israel and making a major contribution to it, is Marcel Dubois, O.P., *Rencontres avec le Judaïsme en Israel* (Jerusalem: Maison St. Isaie, 1983).

On the Canadian dialogue, a special issue of the journal, *Ecumenism* (No. 94, June 1989), edited by Katherine MacDonald, NDS, discusses the issues of *Eretz Israel,* the Shoah, the messiah, salvation, and intermarriage.

Dialogues have more recently begun to proliferate in Latin America as well. One recent example was co-sponsored by the Latin American Bishops' Conference (CELAM) and the ADL. The papers, in English and Spanish, have been published by CELAM (Bogota, Doc. No. 109, 1989), under the title *Desarrollo Humano y Crecimiento Economico,* edited by Peter Berger and Leon Klenicki.

On the European scene, I would mention the 1974–75 Concilium

volume edited by Hans Küng and Walter Kasper, *Christians and Jews*
(N.Y.: Crossroad/Seabury, 1975). This collection pairs articles by Chris-
tian and Jewish thinkers on the following topics (with an interesting
introduction by Küng): The Law (Louis Jacobs, Wm. Davies), Liturgy
(Joseph Heinemann, Clemens Thoma), Religiousness (Samuel Sandmel,
Jan Milie Lochman), Messianic Hope (Jakob Petuchowski, Jürgen Molt-
mann), Jesus (David Flusser, Bernard Dupuy), and "The Future of the
Dialogue" (Uriel Tal, Kurt Hruby).

Also in this category is *Encountering Jesus-Encountering Judaism*
(N.Y.: Crossroad, 1987), which records an extended conversation between Karl Rahner and Pinchas Lapide.

2. THE NEW TESTAMENT AND JUDAISM

The works reviewed in this category were produced within the last
few years. Though written from a variety of critical perspectives, and by
Protestant, Catholic and Jewish scholars, they mark an historic watershed
in New Testament studies. Together, they present a definitive challenge
to the academic biases of our anti-Judaic past and open the way for a
completely fresh approach to the events of the first century, the importance of which cannot be overstated.

E.P. Sanders' *Paul and Palestinian Judaism* (Philadelphia: Fortress,
1977) not only synthesizes the work of the pioneers in this field (G.F.
Moore, James Parkes and others), but virtually demolishes many of the
most cherished assumptions Christian scholars still falsely hold about the
nature of Judaism. He establishes beyond doubt that Rabbinic Judaism
was neither a religion of salvation through works ("works-righteousness")
in the Protestant sense of these terms, nor entrapped in legalism. Rather,
Judaism's "covenantal nomism" is far different from the view Christians
normally impose on it. Unlike the German scholars he critiques, Sanders
has a command of the primary sources that enables him to see why basic
terms, such as sin, law, righteousness and even salvation have significantly different meanings in the two traditions.

Sanders performs a similar service for those grappling with the gospel traditions about Jesus, in *Jesus and Judaism* (Fortress, 1985) which
meticulously rebuts common scholarly misperceptions of first-century
Judaism and offers in their place a well-reasoned historical reconstruction of Jesus in the context of his times.

Anti-Judaism in Christian Theology by Charlotte Klein, N.D.S.,
(Phila.: Fortress, 1978) is a critical survey of the portrayal of Judaism in a

wide range of European (again, especially German) scholarship. She brings into stark relief the ignorance of, and even prejudice against, Jews on the part of such major figures as Guardini, Noth, Bultmann, Dibelius, Schurer, Wellhausen, Lagrange, Bonsirven, Jeremias, Kittle and Strack-Billerbeck. Most of what we "learn" about Judaism from these sources, she shows, is at best misleading and often severely distorted.

Father Gerard Sloyan's provocative *Is Christ the End of the Law?* (Philadelphia: Westminster, 1978) provides the material for a major revision of traditional Christian understandings of our relationship with Torah. Sloyan surveys the many differing views of "law" found in the New Testament and later patristic works. Since "the same God is author of both testaments," he holds, the Mosaic law and Christ, as means of grace, "cannot be mutually exclusive."

Two of the last works by the distinguished Jewish scholar, Samuel Sandmel, also need mention here. *Judaism and Christian Beginnings* (N.Y.: Oxford University Press, 1978) provides a definitive textbook for presenting the emergence of Christianity from synagogue Judaism. Sandmel surveys the sources, institutions and ideas of the richly complex world of first-century Judaism in clear, readable style. His introduction of rabbinic thought and style captures beautifully the inner world of the Talmud and sets the scene for an honest appraisal of the New Testament in its original setting.

Anti-Semitism in the New Testament? (Phila.: Fortress, 1978) provides a frank, sensitive approach to an exceedingly difficult issue. Sandmel takes the reader book by book through the New Testament. He shows convincingly that there are anti-Jewish elements embedded in the apostolic writings, and indeed that some of the authors engaged in a strong apologetic against Judaism in their use of the oral and liturgical materials from which they built their accounts. On the other hand, he maintains, anti-Semitism is neither an essential nor an irremovable aspect of Christianity.

It is the last affirmation that distinguishes Sandmel's approach from that of Rosemary Radford Ruether in her controversial *Faith and Fratricide: The Theological Roots of Anti-Semitism* (Seabury, 1974). There, Ruether appears to argue that anti-Semitism as such emerged as the "left hand of Christology" as reflected within the New Testament, so that a frighteningly straight historical line can be drawn from the apostolic writings to the Nazi death camps.

This theory has been strongly challenged, the most strenuous of which is John Oesterreicher's *Anatomy of Contempt* (Seton Hall University, 1975). The fact that the New Testament authors engaged in various polemics against rabbinic Judaism as it and the church developed side by side in the wake of the destruction of the Temple is increasingly conceded by most scholars. Oesterreicher also takes on Martin Buber in *The Unfinished Dialogue* (N.Y.: Philosophical Library, 1986), though with greater respect and deference.

Historian Yosef Hayim Yerushalmi's trenchant response to Ruether in the volume, *Auschwitz: Beginning of a New Era?* (Cathedral Church of St. John the Divine, KTAV, ADL, 1977), points out a number of historical variables that Ruether's "straight line" theory fails to take into account: "Even if we grant that Christian teaching was a necessary course leading to the Holocaust, it was surely not a sufficient one. . . . There must be some significance in the fact that the Holocaust took place in our secular century, and *not* in the Middle Ages" (p. 103). Other seminal essays in this volume edited by Eva Fleischner include Irving Greenberg's "Cloud of Smoke, Pillar of Fire," Gregory Baum's "Rethinking the Church's Mission After Auschwitz," and Emil Fackenheim's "The Holocaust and the State of Israel", all with important responses. The volume thus remains a classic in the field.

Ruether's more recent summary of her position in an essay in the volume *Jews and Christians After the Holocaust,* edited by Abraham J. Peck (Fortress, 1982), interestingly, does not draw upon her earlier historical theory, though it does not in any way back down from her basic challenge that christology itself needs to be rethought today in order to avoid its abuse as a possible excuse for anti-Semites. For this position, as we shall see below, there is increasing support among a wide range of scholars.

Also reacting to the positions taken in *Faith and Fraticide* are the twelve essays by major Christian scholars in *Antisemitism and the Foundations of Christianity* (A.T. Davies, ed., Paulist, 1979). These tackle the question of the extent to which the New Testament and patristic authors allowed anti-Jewish polemics to color their writings, and how we ought to react in our theological reflections today. John Townsend, for example, notes that the treatment of *ha Ioudaioi* (normally, but not always aptly translated as "the Jews") correlated quite well with passages scholars for independent reasons date to various stages of the gospel's development. In the earlier stages, the gospel uses the term in neutral or positive theological contexts (e.g., "Salvation is from the Jews"). It is only in the later stages, reflecting the increasing bitterness of the split between Jews and Christians, that the phrase takes on its definite polemical edge. (cf. the essays by New Testament scholars Gerard Sloyan and Pinchas Lapide in *Face to Face*'s special issue, "The Parting of the Ways," 1982, for an update of recent scholarship on John's gospel and Luke-Acts). Which of the various theologies of Judaism presented in the New Testament is to be chosen today is, of course, a matter of hermeneutics more than pure exegesis. In this regard Davies, in his introduction, summarizes an emerging consensus among Christian theologians who have dealt with the question.

If a common motif in these essays can be described, it is the conviction that Christians need not choose between

> an ideological defense of their scriptures that wards off damaging criticism and the sad conclusion that the New Testament is so wholly contaminated by anti-Jewish prejudice as to lose all moral authority. Instead, through careful study, Christians can isolate what genuine forms of anti-Judaism really color the major writings and, by examining their historic genesis, neutralize their potential for harm (p. xv).

Or, as Gregory Baum trenchantly puts the case in his "Catholic Dogma After Auschwitz" in the same volume:

> The traditional teaching [of contempt] stands condemned by a superior principle, namely the redemption of human life, which constitutes the spirit and substance of the Bible. . . . Because of this supreme biblical teaching, it is possible to correct certain positions of scripture and tradition when they serve the destruction of life and the enslavement of human beings (pp. 140–141).

Baum's approach is quite similar in tone to the framing of the question by David Tracy in the Peck volume (below, part 9), where he calls for a "Catholic hermeneutics of suspicion, based on a recognition of ambiguities in the tradition alongside (not replacing) a hermeneutics of retrieval based on a fundamental trust in the tradition." In a similar spirit, Jorge Mejia of the Vatican's Commission for Religious Relations with the Jews in his contribution to the *Biblical Studies* volume (below, part 4), emphasizes that "we have (in Catholic tradition) a set of hermeneutical rules which go well beyond the boundaries of scientific exegesis." For Mejia and other Roman Catholic thinkers, the teaching of the magisterium, for example in *Nostra Aetate,* while it cannot stand outside the essential biblical critique, can "become normative and give the right clue for the interpretation of difficult passages like 1 Thes. 2:14–16 and others" (*Biblical Studies,* p. 60). Such an approach allows the Catholic preacher, as Raymond Brown affirms (if I read him correctly) in his *Community of the Beloved Disciples* (Paulist, 1977) to proclaim the gospels, anti-Jewish polemical warts and all, in the liturgy, and yet use the pulpit to proclaim the non-binding, historically conditioned character of those same polemical passages.

This approach to New Testament polemics, it might be noted, appears to be distinctively Roman Catholic in its hermeneutical emphasis on the dynamic tension it would maintain between scripture and tradition. One might expect Protestant approaches, well exemplified in the volumes reported on here, to have greater difficulties with the hermeneutics issue. It is a mark of the progress in ecumenical relations, therefore, to be able to note, that while appeals to tradition are naturally not as discernable among Protestants, a range of creative hermeneutical approaches is being developed which offers hope for the future and to which Catholics can look for inspiration.

At one end of the spectrum, surely, is Norman A. Beck's *Mature Christianity: The Recognition and Repudiation of the Anti-Jewish Polemic of the New Testament* (London and Toronto: Associated University Presses, 1985). The other end of the spectrum can be represented by Luke T. Johnson's "The N.T.'s Anti-Jewish Slander and the Conventions of Ancient Polemic" in *Journal of Biblical Literature* (108/3, 1989) 419–441, which finesses the contemporary hermeneutical dilemma by citing similar passages of ancient rhetoric, implying that the N.T. polemics should not be taken seriously. Perhaps not, but they have been for two millennia and remain so today.

Lutheran scholar John Koenig's more balanced (though less exhaustive) *Jews and Christians in Dialogue: New Testament Foundations* (Westminster, 1979), deals forthrightly and frankly with the polemic strands embedded in various New Testament traditions, but also raises up for reflection elements of New Testament traditions on which a more positive theology of the Christian-Jewish relationship can be built.

Another Protestant scholar, Clark M. Williamson of Christian Theological Seminary, has produced a book which I hope will find wide readership among all Christians. *Has God Rejected His People?* (Abingdon, 1982) poses the central biblical and theological challenges in concise, readable fashion that makes it useful for pastors and adult discussion groups alike.

Williamson applies his approach for Christian preachers and teachers in *When Jews and Christians Meet* (St. Louis: CBP Press, 1989) and in *Interpreting Difficult Texts: Anti-Judaism and Christian Preaching* (Philadelphia: Trinity Press, 1989), with Ronald J. Allin.

One of the most enduring elements of the traditional Christian teaching of contempt centers on a polemical treatment of the Pharisees in the gospels, especially Matthew (Luke/Acts, on the other hand, shows Pharisees trying to save Jesus' life and succeeding in saving the lives of the apostles), and the projection of that negative portrait onto later rabbinic Judaism as a whole. Ellis Rivkin's controversial *The Hidden Revolution: The Pharisees' Search for the Kingdom Within* (Abingdon, 1978), turns around many of our presuppositions about this group of deeply spiritual leaders by analyzing carefully the information we actually possess on them from ancient contemporary literature.

Also challenging, and likely to be controversial, is Harvey Falk's *Jesus the Pharisee* (Paulist, 1985). Falk, an Orthodox Rabbi, argues that Jesus was close to the views of the Beth Hillel school of Pharisees, joining them in denouncing the Shammaites. It was the latter, along with the Temple party, that acted in concert with Pilate to bring about his death. See also Asher Finkel's earlier *The Pharisees and the Teacher of Nazareth* (Leiden: Brill, 1964) on the Hillel/Shammai division in relation to Jesus' teaching.

The critical importance for Christian theology of a more open appreciation of the impact of Pharisaic/Rabbinic thought on Christian tradition has been well chronicled in the works of John T. Pawlikowski, beginning with his *Sinai and Calvary* (Benzinger, 1976) and continuing through his *Christ in the Light of the Christian-Jewish Dialogue* (Paulist, Stimulus Books, 1982), where Pharisaism is seen as a "key to Christological Understanding" (pp. 76–107). Pawlikowski is forced to stretch the evidence a bit to come up with distinctions between Jesus' teaching and that of the Pharisees. Jesus' "Abba experience," for example, is just that and not a teaching at all, and the *am ha-aretz* do not represent "the poor" as an "outcast" class as Pawlikowski would have it. The *Mishna,* rather, uses the term solely with reference to peoples' reliability in ritual matters. Unreliable priests, for example, are included in the category. (See K.N. Rengstart, "La martolos," in TDNT 1. 317–35 and Johnson, *cit.,* 438). The positive pole of Pawlikowski's description of "Pharisaic Influences on Jesus" in this chapter is both remarkably refreshing and theologically provocative, as is his updated survey of the literature in *Jesus and the Theology of Israel* (Wilmington, DE: Michael Glazier, Inc., 1989) 48–70.

Christ in the Light, incidentally, is one of several volumes included in this survey sponsored, through Paulist Press, by the Stimulus Foundation, as part of the ongoing series "Studies in Judaism and Christianity." The whole field of Christian-Jewish dialogue, I believe, has been greatly enhanced by the consistently high quality of this eminent series.

Jacob Neusner's and Philip Culbertson's essays on the Pharisees in the October, 1982, issue of *Anglican Theological Review* (Vol. 64, No. 4), devoted entirely to Christian-Jewish relations, provide excellent summaries of the major questions and literature in the field of Pharisaic studies. Similarly, Robin Scroggs provides an overview of recent scholarly inquiry into the Jewishness of Jesus and his teaching in "The Judaizing of the New Testament," *Chicago Theological Seminary Register* (Winter, 1986) 36–45. The two sets of issues, of course, are tightly interwoven, as the treatment of both in the 1985 Vatican *Notes* illustrates so very well.

Also falling into the general category of Jesus' Jewishness and rabbinic thought are the following volumes: *The Gospels and Rabbinic Judaism: A Study Guide* (N.Y.: KTAV and ADL, 1988), by Michael Hilton and Gordian Marshall, take the reader profitably through a series of New Testament and Talmudic texts, and can serve as an excellent resource for dialogue. Pinchas Lapide's *The Sermon on the Mount* (Maryknoll, N.Y.: Orbis, 1986), translated by Arlene Swidler, goes through the text of Matthew 5 passage by passage from a Jewish point of view. Samuel Tobias Lachs' *A Rabbinic Commentary on the New Testament* (N.Y.: KTAV and ADL, 1987), while at times overeager in its parallels, is also handy to have on one's desk when dealing with particular passages from the synoptic gospels.

Terence Callan's *Forgetting the Root: The Emergence of Christianity from Judaism* (Paulist, 1986) analyzes the books of the N.T. on the basis of their relative "liberal" or "conservative" reactions to the issue of Gentile inclusion into the Christian community. The results are often surprising but very helpful for a renewed understanding of the original intent of the sacred texts.

Philip A. Cunningham again synthesizes a wealth of recent scholarly insight into popular form in *Jesus and the Evangelists* (Paulist, 1980), while Bernard J. Lee, S.M., employs empirical-historical methodology to retrieve *The Galilean Jewishness of Jesus* (Paulist/Stimulus, 1988) in the first of a projected three-volume study. Leonard Swidler's *Yeshua: A Model for Moderns* (Kansas City, MO: Sheed and Ward, 1988) has an excellent chapter on this topic (pp. 42–74), but is somewhat problematical in his treatment of theological pluralism and "Yeshua, Feminist and Androgynous." Jacob Neusner's *Christian Faith and the Bible of Ju-*

daism (Grand Rapids, MI: Eerdmans, 1987) illustrates how Jewish tradition reads Genesis, Leviticus and Numbers through selected rabbinic texts. James. H. Charlesworth's *Jesus Within Judaism* (N.Y.: Doubleday, 1988) discusses the results of archaeological discoveries, such as the Dead Sea Scrolls, the Nag Hammadi Codices, and the pseudepigrapha, with reference to "the historical Jesus" and Jesus' "self-understanding."

Lutheran scholar E.P. Sanders' *Paul and Palestianian Judaism* (Fortress, 1977) remains the most thorough dismantling of typical Christian scholarly misinterpretations of rabbinic literature available. No work in the field today can afford to ignore the analysis provided in Part One of this book, though the second part, on Paul himself, leaves many questions unanswered.

Sanders picks up several of these questions in *Paul, the Law, and the Jewish People* (Fortress, 1983), which deals with the purpose of the Law for Paul as reflected especially in Romans and Galatians. Paul's criticism of Judaism ("the Law"), Sanders argues, focuses on christology and equality (in Christ) for the Gentiles, not on a demolition of the Law as such as many scholars have mistakenly presumed. The issue is not "Christian universalism" versus "Jewish particularism," for Paul's insistence on acceptance of Christ as *the* entryway into God's people established its own particularist view of election. Sanders presents Paul as a man deeply troubled by some of the logical conclusions of his own convictions. These internal doubts of Paul's surface in Romans 7 and 9–11, as he says:

> (Paul) was a loyal member of the synagogue. . . . He saw himself as helping to fulfill God's eternal plan, already announced in Genesis, but he was thereby pushing the Christian movement toward becoming a third entity. He knew that righteousness is only by faith in Christ, but he still tried repeatedly to find a place for the Law in God's plan. The most poignant point is the last one considered: he desperately sought a formula which would keep God's promises intact, while insisting on faith in Jesus Christ (p. 199).

Four other works can shed further light on the Epistles (along with the appropriate sections in the previously-mentioned volumes by John Koenig and A.T. Davies—the latter being a most helpful essay on "Paul and the Torah" by Lloyd Gaston (of the Vancouver School of Theology). First, there is Krister Stendahl's *Paul Among the Jews and Gentiles* (Fortress, 1976) which offers the general reader intriguing insights into the Epistles. Stendahl shows that taking Paul's letters out of their original context has led to serious misunderstanding of his intent. Paul did not intend to attack the Law as such, nor to deny its validity for Jews. Rather, he was constructing a theological rationale to justify the direct conversion of Gentiles to Christ without the necessity of their prior conversion to Judaism. Law and gospel are thus not contradictory but complementary terms for Paul, as Stendahl's analysis of Romans 9–11 shows.

Second, Lloyd Gaston's *Paul and the Torah* (Vancouver: University of British Columbia Press, 1987) expands his 1979 article into a major contribution in the field, one which no Pauline scholar should be without.

Third, Philip A. Cunningham's *Jewish Apostle to the Gentiles* (Mystic, CT: Twenty-Third Publications, 1986) synthesizes recent Pauline scholarship into a coherent, popular-level portrait of "Paul as he saw himself." Paul does not challenge the validity of Torah for the Jews but argues that Christ as "the end of the Law" is "the confirmation of all the Torah's promises regarding the salvation of the Gentiles" (p. 70).

Fourth, Jesuit scholar Daniel Harrington's *God's People in Christ: New Testament Perspectives on the Church and Judaism* (Fortress, 1980) is another work that is "must reading" for all interested in early Christian-Jewish relations. Harrington takes an admirably objective view of the evidence and produces a work that illustrates how a non-polemical approach by Christian scholars to Jewish materials of the first centuries can not only help to correct old misunderstandings, but also greatly enrich our understanding of the nature of the early church. Also illustrating the enriched depth of understanding that can come from an appreciation of Jewish sources is Gerard Sloyan's *Jesus in Focus: A Life in Its Setting* (Twenty-Third Publications, 1983) which is both readable and illuminating.

Harrington, in what is something of a *tour de force,* has contributed the introductory volumes to both the Old and the New Testament series of publisher Michael Glazier's ambitious project of Catholic commentaries on all of the books of the canon. This series, written by top biblical scholars on a popular level is, throughout, remarkably free of the older, polemical assumptions of Christian scholars in depicting Jewish themes, making it an excellent example of the constructive bent of mainstream scholarship today. Of particular interest will be Sean Freyne's creative and thoughtful *The World of the New Testament* (Glazier, 1980), which sets the development of the apostolic writings within the context of sensitive understanding of the rich complexity of the Jewish movements of the time. Also highly commendable in the series are the volumes by Lawrence Boadt on Jeremiah, Donald Senior on 1 and 2 Peter, and Eugene Maly on Romans.

In between his two major works on Paul, Sanders has edited two volumes of essays for Fortress Press (1980–1982) under the general title, *Jewish and Christian Self-Definition.* These bring to bear both Jewish and Christian scholarship on key aspects of early Christianity and Judaism and their interrelationships. To give just one example of the richness of these volumes, Reuvin Kimelman's "*Birkat Ha Minim* and the Lack of Evidence for an Anti-Christian Jewish Prayer in Late Antiquity" (Vol. II, 1982, 226–244) punches several well-placed holes in the consensus that had been growing among Christian scholars that the rabbis of the late first century sought to exclude Jewish Christians from the synagogues through the institution of the curse against the *minim* in the Eighteen Benedictions. The evidence, Kimelman points out, is simply insufficient to support the idea. The *minim* would not have included Christians until a much later period; at any rate, not before the age of Constantine and the beginnings of systematic Christian suppression of the Jewish community.

If the Nobel Prize is to be awarded Kimelman for this research, however, he will have to share it with another scholar, Asher Finkel of Seton Hall University, who published, almost simultaneously, an excellent article on the subject entitled "Yavneh's Liturgy and Early Christianity" in the Spring, 1981, issue of the *Journal of Ecumenical Studies,* coming to similar conclusions. Indeed, the fact that (as we shall see) even in Chrysostom's time, some generations *after* Constantine, Christians were knowingly and warmly welcomed into the synagogue, makes the notion of a first-century "expulsion" of Christians from the synagogue highly unlikely. It may be that the references in John's gospel to such an event (which are about the only reliable evidence we have) refer to an actual, local event suffered by the Johannine community. But that, on the evidence as a whole, would have to be considered an isolated occurrence, not ascribable to "the rabbis" or "the synagogue" as a whole. Most recently, Steven T. Katz of Dartmouth has reconsidered the evidence regarding "The Separation of Judaism and Christianity after 70 C.E." (*Journal of Biblical Literature* 103/1 [1984] 43–76.) His conclusion, carefully drawn, is that there exists *no* solid evidence, Christian or Jewish, that there was an "official anti-Christian policy at Yavneh or elsewhere before the Bar Kochba revolt and not total separation between Jews and Christians before . . . the Bar Kochba revolt" (p. 76). Still holding on to the older view, however, is William Herburg in "The Benediction of the *Minim* and Early Jewish-Christian Controversy," *Journal of Theological Studies* 33 (1982) 19–61.

In a real service to the dialogue in this country, Leonard Swidler has translated Franz Mussner's *Tractate on the Jews* (Fortress, 1984). Mussner emphasizes the positive relationship between Jesus and the Law and, based on a close reading of Romans 9–11, lays the foundation for a Christian affirmation of Judaism, *post Christum,* on its own terms rather than as a mere object of conversionism. George W.E. Nickelsburg and Michael E. Stone provide an excellent selection of source material in translation from the Second Temple period in *Faith and Piety in Early Judaism: Texts and Documents* (Fortress, 1983). The texts are arranged in six general categories: Sects and Parties, Temple and Cult, Ideals of Piety, Deliverance and Judgment, Agents of Divine Deliverance, Lady Wisdom and Israel. Each section is introduced with a solid discussion of the overall issues, and each is helpfully annotated. Since New Testament passages are included alongside other topically related documents of Second Temple Judaism, the reader is enabled to discern the place of early Christianity within its natural and dynamically vibrant Jewish milieu.

Likewise, Roger le Déaut's excellent introduction to the *Targums* for Christians (Aramaic paraphrases of the Bible) has been translated by S.F. Miletic under the title, *The Message of the New Testament and the Aramaic Bible* (Rome: Biblical Institute Press, 1982), in an expanded, updated edition from the French original. For Christians, the discovery of learning to read the Bible through the prism of Jewish Traditions, Le Déaut shows, can be a fascinating and enriching experience.

No survey of recent Christian literature on the New Testament and Judaism would be complete without a contribution from W.D. Davies, whose classic works, *Paul and Rabbinic Judaism* (Fortress Press) and *The Setting of the Sermon on the Mount* (Cambridge University Press, 1966), have been a measure of the field. Davies' latest collection of key essays, written by the author between the early 1960s and the early 1980s, with one essay (on Josephus) dating from 1954, is *Jewish and Pauline Studies* (Fortress, 1984). Substantial additions to the text and notes update the essays and give Davies' reactions to many of the works dealt with here.

A number of Davies' essays deal with the concept of law in first-century Judaism, Paul and the New Testament in general. Related essays probe the question of moral teaching in the New Testament and Paul's views on Jews and Gentiles. Especially illuminating in this latter regard are his trenchant insights into key texts of Romans and Galatians. Davies' more direct studies of Judaica include reflections on Tradition ('*Abot*), the territorial dimension of Judaism (a handy summary of his lengthier *The Gospel and the Land*), and on "the Spirit in the Mekilta."

Summing up the discussion to date of the Ruether thesis and making its own creative contribution to our understanding of both St. Paul and church history up to the early fourth century, is John G. Gager's *The Origins of Anti-Semitism: Attitudes Toward Judaism in Pagan and Christian Antiquity* (Oxford University Press, 1983). Gager first sets the anti-Jewish sayings of pagan antiquity into the wider context of equally prevalent neutral and positive attitudes toward Jewish tradition on the part of Greeks and Romans. This helps to correct exaggerated notions about how widespread "anti-Semitism" (an anachronism as Gager rightly points out) was within the ancient world. Rather, Judaism emerges as surprisingly attractive for many pagans, with the purity of its monotheism and the antiquity (even then) of its practice. "Judaizing" was common among the ancients long before their acceptance of Christianity. One cannot, then, fudge the question of *Christian* anti-Semitism merely by pointing to pagan anti-Jewish precedent. The real picture is vastly more complex.

Gager does an equally effective job of putting both Christian and Pauline thought back into their wider historical context, dispelling many myths there as well. Gager acknowledges that for Paul, "Torah and Christ are mutually exclusive categories," but concludes that, equally for Paul, "the relationship between the two is such that neither invalidates the other. Torah remains the path of righteousness for Israel; Christ has become the promised way of righteousness for Gentiles" (p. 247).

3. THE TRIAL OF JESUS

This is a critical subtopic of the wider issue presented above. My own *Faith without Prejudice* (Paulist, 1977) provides a brief introduction to it in chapter four. Donald Juel's *Messiah and Temple* (Scholars Press, Missoula, Mont., 1977) shows that the account in chapter 26 of Matthew of a Sanhedrin trial is a literary device rather than strict history in our modern sense of the term.

Haim Cohen's *The Trial and Death of Jesus,* reissued by KTAV (N.Y.: 1977) argues that there was no "Jewish trial" of Jesus at all, but only the Roman one by Pilate. While Cohen's theory that the Jewish leaders involved did so to save the life of Jesus is highly speculative, his presentation of the Jewish and Roman legal material bearing on the question is an excellent resource.

Also reissued, and still of interest, is S.G.F. Brandon's *The Trial of Jesus of Nazareth* (Stein and Day, A Scarborough Book, 1979). Brandon, like Juel, asks the question whether the gospel accounts of the trial as we have them, with their many internal and external contradictions, should be considered "history or theology." The earliest version, Mark's, Brandon notes, "was an apologetical interpretation" in a Roman-Christian setting of an earlier apologetical tradition, probably Jerusalemite. Mark solves the "scandal of the Roman cross" for his fellow Roman Christians by structuring the account within his gospel to point the finger at a Jewish conspiracy.

The literature on this subject is now becoming extensive. Gerard Sloyan in *Jesus on Trial* (Fortress, 1973) surveys the historical and biblical questions. A variety of both Jewish and Christian views are found in the special issue of *Judaism* (Vol. 20, No. 1, Winter 1971). For recent surveys of the literature, see J. Fitzmyer, "Jesus the Lord" in *Chicago Studies 17* (1978) 87–90 and *A Christological Catechism* (Paulist, 1982); and G. Sloyan, "Recent Literature on the Trial Narratives" in T.J. Ryan, ed., *Critical History and Biblical Faith* (Villanova University: College Theology Society, 1979) 136–176. J. Pawlikowski's chapter on "The Deicide Charge and New Testament Antisemitism" in his *What Are They Saying About Christian-Jewish Relations?* (Paulist, 1980, pp. 1–32) provides perhaps the most succinct and approachable introduction to the theological implications of the questions raised in this and the previous section. Pawlikowski surveys critically Jewish and Christian reconstructions of the events of "The Trial and Death of Jesus" in *Chicago Studies* (Vol. 33, No. 1, April 1986) 79–94.

John T. Townsend's *A Liturgical Interpretation of Our Lord's Passion in Narrative Form* (N.Y.: National Conference of Christians and Jews, 1985) is the product of the combined efforts of a group of Catholic and Protestant scholars known as the Israel Study Group. The resulting booklet should be of immense value to liturgists, homilists and educators. Offered is a paraphrase of the gospel passion narratives designed for public reading, along with extensive notes giving a solid biblical-historical understanding of the actual events as they are reconstructed today by the best of modern scholarship. An accompanying pamphlet, prepared by liturgist Gabe Huck for NCCJ, now arranges the reading in dramatic form. An example of official application of recent scholarly research in this area is *Criteria for the Evaluation of Dramatizations of the Passion* (Washington, D.C. 1988) issued by the Bishops' Committee for Ecumenical and Interreligious Affairs. It is designed for parish use and for those putting on Passion Plays.

4. THE RELATIONSHIP BETWEEN THE SCRIPTURES

In his important address to representatives of the German-Jewish community in Mainz, Pope John Paul II noted that the dialogue "between the people of God of the old covenant never retracted by God, on the one hand, and the people of the new covenant, on the other, is at the same time a dialogue within our own Church, so to speak, a dialogue between the first and second part of its Bible" (Nov. 17, 1980). In other words, those who see the New Testament as "abrogating" the Old, or reduce the Hebrew scriptures to a mere preparation ("propaedeutic" in the pejorative term favored by Bultmann), will tend to have negative or ambiguous attitudes toward Jews and Judaism, at least on the level of religious theory. Conversely, to respect the integrity of Hebrew scriptures as God's word for us today is to move to a position of least potential dissonance between the church and the Jewish people in the spirit that the pope termed "mutual esteem."

Joseph Blenkinsopp's masterful essay, "Tanakh and New Testament" in the Stimulus volume *Biblical Studies: Meeting Ground of Jews and Christians* (Paulist, 1980) poses the major biblical question quite aptly. After surveying major Christian efforts at producing systematic "Old Testament theologies," Blenkinsopp writes:

> If the general impression conveyed in this essay is overwhelmingly negative, and if we have said little positively about the relation between Old and New Testament, we can only plead that we [Christians] are as yet nowhere close to knowing how to write an Old Testament theology. It seems that first we must take Tanakh seriously on its own terms which, given the way it came into existence, involves coming to terms with the Second Temple period inclusive of early Christianity as a phenomenon of Second Temple Palestinian Judaism. It involves further, as necessary consequence, coming to terms historically and theologically with Judaism which, far from declining or disappearing at the time of early Christianity, only reached its most characteristic expressions several centuries later (p. 113).

The *Biblical Studies* volume which contains important essays also by Lawrence Boadt, C.S.P. (a co-editor with Leon Klenicki and Helga Croner), Andre Lacocque, and Monika Hellwig, appears to begin this process quite well. In an essay on "The Impact of the Christian-Jewish Dialogue on Biblical Studies" in Richard Rosseau, S.J., ed., *Christianity and Judaism: The Deepening Dialogue* (Ridge Row Press, 1983, pp. 117–138), Eugene Fisher surveys hermeneutical challenges and exegetical enrichments emerging from the recent, more dialogically open approach taken today within the biblical critical enterprise as a whole. Boadt offers a complementary survey of "The Role of Scripture in Catholic-Jewish Relations" in Fisher, Rudin, Tanenbaum, *Twenty Years* (cf., Section One, above, pp. 89–108).

Four essays from *Face to Face*'s special issue on the Rainbow Group, an interfaith dialogue group of scholars in Jerusalem (N.Y.: ADL, Vol. 10, Fall 1983) should also be mentioned in this biblical section: "Theses on the Emergence of Christianity from Judaism," by David Flusser; "Christian Misreadings of Hebrew Scriptures," by Walter Harrelson; "The Marcionite Approach to the Bible," by Joseph Stiassney; and "The Hebrew Bible—A Common Source," by J. (Coos) Schoneveld.

A highly significant analysis and critique of *Heilsgeschichte* (Sacred History) as a principle of biblical theology for relating the scriptures is offered by Mary C. Boys in *Biblical Interpretation in Religious Education* (Birmingham, AL: Religious Education Press, 1980).

For a summary of many of the above points on the popular level (for preachers, teachers, and adult discussion groups), see Eugene Fisher, *Faith Without Prejudice: Rebuilding Christian Attitudes Toward Judaism* (Paulist, 1977, chapters 2–4). On a more scholarly level, the biblical and theological challenges are surveyed in Eugene Fisher, *Seminary Education and Christian-Jewish Relations* (Washington, D.C.: National Catholic Educational Association, 1988). That volume also contains suggestions for seminary educators, liturgy, church history, catechetics and field education.

5. THE PATRISTIC PERIOD

While the New Testament reflects a developing conflict between church and synagogue, studies of the writings of the early fathers of the church reveal an open split in some areas as early as the second century.

Samuele Bacchiocchi's *From Sabbath to Sunday* (Rome: Pontifical Gregorian University, 1977) investigates the historical origins of the change from Saturday to Sunday observance in the church of Rome. Noting that the New Testament nowhere mandates such a shift, Bacchiocchi (a Seventh-Day Adventist) points to the repressive measures enacted by the Roman emperors against Jews as creating "the necessity of a radical Christian separation from Judaism." To differentiate itself from Judaism, the early church engaged in progressively more hostile and anti-Judaic polemics and sought to distinguish its own rituals as clearly as possible from those, such as the Sabbath, most characteristic of Judaism in pagan eyes. Though several points (especially his treatment of the biblical materials) call for further research, this is an important work for liturgists as well as historians.

An intriguing work written in response to Bacchiocchi is D.A. Carson, ed., *From Sabbath to Lord's Day* (Grand Rapids: Zondervan, 1982). The seven scholars represented in the book originally came together to study the question under a Tyndale Fellowship in 1973, which gives their presentation an internal cohesiveness and completeness not usual in a collection of essays. Dealing with the issue in scripture, history and theological perspective (e.g., its implications for the relationship between the covenants), they conclude that the origins of Sunday observance do indeed go back to New Testament times, but that "it was not perceived as a Christian Sabbath" (p. 16), arguing rather its connection with developing "First Day" or "End-Time" (eschatological) theology.

Other works center specifically on the development of the *verus Israel* traditions ("true Israel" or, as I personally prefer, "truly Israel,") with reference to the church. Theodore Stylianopolous' *Justin Martyr and the Mosaic Law* (Scholars Press, 1975) is a dissertation analyzing Justin's polemic against the Law in the second century. Nicholas de Lange's *Origen and the Jews: Studies in Jewish-Christian Relations in Third Century Palestine* (Cambridge University, 1976) brilliantly outlines both Origen's negative apologetic and his surprising reliance on Jewish exegetical insights in his own work on scripture. Interestingly, we find both Origen and Justin defending "Old Testament" Judaism against pagan and gnostic attacks at the same time. An earlier work, *Judaism and the Early Christian Mind* by R.L. Wilken (Yale University, 1971) gives an excellent overview of the subject, as well as a detailed study of Cyril of Alexandria's quite mistaken belief that Judaism was dying. "The sheer historical fact of the continuation of Judaism after the rise of Christianity," Wilken writes, "is a source of the theological difficulties Christians have had with Jews."

R.L. Wilken's recent *John Chrysostom and the Jews: Rhetoric and*

Reality in the Late 4th Century (University of California Press, 1983) sets Chrysostom's anti-Jewish and anti-Judaic polemics into the larger context of his times. Chrysostom's sermons are seen as fitting into the inflated rhetorical patterns of the time and occasioned, not so much by Jewish-Christian relations or difficulties (he denies, for example, that there is any evidence of Jewish proselytizing of Christians) as by the increasing numbers of Gentile Christians ("Judaizers") attracted to the ritual and lifestyle of Jesus. The Jewish community in Antioch, and throughout much of the ancient world at the time, was relatively large and in ongoing contact with the Christian community. Linked with Emperor Julian's nearly successful attempt to rebuild the Jerusalem Temple (on the destruction of which Christians placed great store as a central "proof" of the accuracy of Jesus' prophesies and therefore of Christian claims about Jesus) and the anti-Christian polemics of the still dominant pagan culture, Chrysostom's invectives would have been seen, at the time, as defensive rather than essentially aggressive. On the other hand, this is not to condone Chrysostom's excesses of rhetoric, nor to agree with his theology of history, which has, in any case, been shattered by the events of our own century. While, as Wilken concludes, it is unfair to project the attitudes (and despicable deeds) of later Christians toward Jews onto events of the fourth century, "that is no reason why it (Chrysostom's view of the Jews) should be our own view" (p. 164).

An excellent set of essays contributing to our understanding of Christian-Jewish relations in the first through the fourth centuries (and beyond) is found in Jacob Neusner and Ernest Frerichs, eds., *To See Ourselves as Others See Us* (Scholars Press, 1985).

Finally, Notre Dame University's Center for the Study of Judaism and Christianity in Antiquity has come out with two volumes which illustrate the benefits of a dialogue approach to religious scholarship. Elizabeth Schussler Fiorenza, ed., *Religious Propaganda in Judaism and Early Christianity* (1976) and R. Wilken, ed., *Wisdom in Judaism and Early Christianity* (1975).

6. THE MEDIEVAL PERIOD AND THE REFORMATION

The best introduction to works on medieval Jewish-Christian relations remains the collection of annotated bibliographies in ADL's *Bibliographical Essays in Medieval Jewish Studies* (KTAV, 1976). F.E. Talmage's *Disputation and Dialogue* (ADL/KTAV, 1975), likewise remains the handiest collection of documents gathered from across the centuries.

This is a classic anthology that can be highly recommended for student and specialist alike. The selections span the entire history of Jewish-Christian interaction and present samples of both bitter polemic and courageous outreach to the other side of the debate. Both Christian and Jewish works are well-represented, each briefly introduced and set in historical context.

Jewish Philosophical Polemics Against Christianity in the Middle Ages, by D. Lasker (KTAV/ADL, 1977) is a more specialized work. This published version of the author's 1976 dissertation for Brandeis University is included here because of the wide range of thinkers whose work is presented and summarized. It is interesting to note that medieval Jewish polemicists tended to write in Hebrew, directing their arguments, not at Christians, but at Jews, in the hope of providing them with defenses against the influence of conversionary attempts directed at them by Christians.

R. Chazan's *Church, State and Jews in the Middle Ages* (Behrman House, 1980) provides a well-chosen collection of documents ranging from Gratian's *Decretum* to fifteenth-century accounts of the expulsion from Spain. A much more intense view of a single document, the *Nizzahon Vetus,* with critical translation, introduction and commentary, is given in David Berger's scholarly *The Jewish-Christian Debate in the High Middle Ages* (Jewish Publication Society, 1979). The "Old Book of Polemics," as it has come to be known, contains what Berger aptly remarks is "a virtual encyclopedia of Jewish arguments against Christianity." Many of these arguments, it must be noted with some sadness, are still current in some quarters of the Jewish community even today (cf. Fisher, "Typical Jewish Misunderstandings of Christianity," *Judaism,* Winter, 1973).

Edward A. Synan's, *The Popes and the Jews in the Middle Ages* (Macmillan, 1965), though produced too early for proper inclusion in this review, remains so basic to an understanding of the history of the period and the interpretation of papal canonical legislation, that it must be recommended. Complementing it from another point of view (the interplay between sociological and theological factors) is Jeremy Cohen's impressive study, *The Friars and the Jews: The Evolution of Medieval Anti-Judaism* (Cornell University Press, 1983). This work shows how the mendicant orders (Dominicans and Franciscans) beginning in the thirteenth century gradually brought about, in place after place, a new sense of ideological intolerance of Jews and Judaism, contravening and suppressing the centuries-old traditional Christian view that Jews must survive, expressed in papal legislation and in the writings of church fathers, such as Augustine of Hippo. Cohen shows, through analysis of the works of Raymond de Penaforte, Pablo Christiani, Raymond Martini, Nocholas of Lyra and Raymond Lull, how the friars justified in theological terms their efforts to "purge" Europe of its Jewish population. By the sixteenth century, with the notable exception of Poland, they had become largely successful.

Also challenging traditional understandings of medieval Papal-Jewish relations is Kenneth R. Stow's *The "1007 Anonymous" and Papal Sovereignty* (Cincinnati's Hebrew Union College, 1984). In concise fashion, Stow delineates the major elements of papal policy toward the Jews, highlighting their reliability from the contemporary Jewish viewpoint as against the vagaries and vacillations of the medieval kings. Unfortunately, Stow concludes that the kings ignored the teachings of the popes on the place of Jews in society, and in due time went on to exploit and then expel them against the papal will.

Two fine examples of historical research examine individual, but significant aspects of Vatican-Jewish relations. Leon Poliakov surveys the economic and social factors behind this unique, symbiotic relationship from the thirteenth to the seventeenth centuries in *Jewish Bankers and the Holy See* (Boston: Routledge and Kegan Paul, 1978). Interestingly, it appears that the economic relationship was snapped at just about the time that the new, conversionary-oriented policy begun by Paul IV in the late sixteenth century was going into full swing. The theological intent behind this new legal approach to the Jews is set forth in Kenneth Stow's excellent *Catholic Thought and Papal Jewry Policy* (KTAV/JTS, 1977).

A minor, perhaps, but quite illuminating aspect of medieval Christian-Jewish relations is revealed by T. Egido, O.E.C., in a study of "The Historical Setting of St. Teresa's (of Avila) Life" in *Carmelite Studies* annual for 1980 (pp. 122–183). Besides unravelling the Jewish parentage of St. Teresa, Egido describes the life-situations and travails of Spanish "Judeo-converso" families (a term preferable to the old, and many feel, insulting term "Marranos").

Scholars and students of medieval history will be grateful to the Anti-Defamation League of B'nai B'rith for sponsoring the reissue of Joshua Trachtenberg's classic study, *The Devil and the Jews: The Medieval Conception of the Jew and its Relation to Modern Anti-Semitism* (Jewish Publication Society of America, 1983). Through historical sources such as church documents, legal codes, Passion plays, folk tales and the graphic arts, Trachtenberg traces the progressive "demonization" of the Jews from the eleventh to the sixteenth centuries. He is thus able to put in high relief what he calls "the paradox" of medieval Christian policy toward the Jews: "Bitterly condemned and excoriated, they were yet to be tolerated on humanitarian grounds" (p. 164). As Marc Saperstein's Foreword for this new edition asks: The paradox that strikes us most today, "a generation after the Holocaust" is how, given Trachtenberg's depiction of the "demonic conception of the Jew" permeating every layer of Christian society, "the Jews were tolerated at all in Christian countries . . . never made the object of a holy war of extermination as was directed against Christian heretics?" (p. ix). Saperstein notes that the negative portrait of the Jews, documented so well by Trachtenberg, must be seen as "only one aspect of the medieval conception of the Jew," and that further historical work needs to be done to uncover and set in context the "neutral or even positive" understandings of Jews and Judaism which are equally a part of the ambivalent Christian heritage (p. x).

Saperstein's own *Moments of Crisis in Jewish-Christian Relations* (Phila.: Trinity Press, 1989) surveys the historical issues in antiquity, the Middle Ages, the Reformation, and the Holocaust. The latter is perhaps too recent for Saperstein as an historian to gain the desired distance and objectivity. Saperstein apparently believes that Pope Pius XII could simply have "said the word" and Nazism would have abandoned the final solution, a remarkably simplistic view in an otherwise sophisticated and distinguished volume.

An intensive look at one medieval development still threatening Christian-Jewish relations after 350 years is provided in Saul S. Friedman's *The Oberammergau Passion Play* (Southern Illinois Univ. Press, 1984), which also describes contemporary efforts to revise the play.

In *The Jew as Ally of the Muslim* (University of Notre Dame Press, 1986), Allan and Helen Cutler argue that it was association of Jews with Muslims in the minds of medieval Christians that led to the tragic change in policy toward Jews in the High Middle Ages, a change noted by Cohen, Stow, and others above. The argument has merit, I believe, though the authors attempt to explain too much with their single thesis.

In the *Roots of Antisemitism in the Age of Renaissance and Reformation* (Fortress, 1984), the great Luther scholar, Heiko Oberman, shows the links between the medieval and modern periods in the development of anti-Judaic theory and practice within Christianity. Though the reformers critically challenged most elements of their medieval heritage, anti-Jewishness was not, in the end, one of them.

An excellent overall depiction of the period up to the eve of the

Enlightenment is provided by John Edwards' *The Jews in Christian Europe* (London and New York: Routledge, 1989). Dedicated to the memory of W.W. Simpson, one of the great Anglican pioneers of the dialogue, Edwards' volume is a fitting tribute to that great ecumenist and an excellent survey of its subject.

7. THE MODERN PERIOD: JEWS AND CHRISTIANS IN AMERICA

The bicentennial year prompted a surge of studies on the Jewish experience in and contribution to America. Abraham I. Katsch's *The Biblical Heritage of American Democracy* (KTAV, 1977), is filled with fascinating reading on how the outlook of colonial America was decisively influenced by the "the legacy of Judaism," especially that of the Hebrew scriptures.

Simon Greenberg's *The Ethical in the Jewish and American Heritage* (KTAV/JTS, 1977) attempts to trace the affinities and interaction between Jewish and American historical experience. His presentation of how ethics and law function in Judaism will be of special interest to the Christian reader.

The summer, 1978, issue of *Judaism* is an invaluable introduction to Jewish-Christian relations as they exist in America today. Titled "Interfaith at Fifty," the collection of essays by Jewish, Catholic and Protestant leaders both celebrated the golden anniversary of the National Conference of Christians and Jews and assesses the history and future of the dialogue.

John Murray Cuddihy's *No Offense: Civil Religion and Protestant Taste* (Seabury, 1978), is a book to enjoy and to debate with close friends. Cuddihy deals with the clash between self-sufficient traditionalism and pluralistic modernism among American Catholics, Protestants and Jews. He does this in terms of individuals, chiefly John Courtney Murray, Reinhold Niebuhr and Arthur Hertzberg. Episodic and rich in texture, this book will often exasperate and illuminate, usually both at the same time.

For those wishing to live, or relive, the experiences endured by Jews immigrating to America, Irving Howe's bestselling *World of Our Fathers* (Harcourt, Brace, Jovanovich, 1976) remains a highly readable narrative.

Esther Yolles Feldblum's excellent *The American Catholic Press and the Jewish State 1917–1959* (KTAV, 1977), traces Catholic reactions to the Zionist ideal from the period of the Balfour Declaration to the Second Vatican Council. Well-balanced and insightful, it chronicles the transition from an age of triumphalism to one of exciting dialogue.

With hate groups such as the KKK seemingly on the rise, it is important to look back to where we have come from in this country. Nathan Belth's *A Promise to Keep* (ADL/Times Books, 1979) illustrates the fact that upsurges in anti-Semitism have traditionally been associated with rises in nativist, anti-Catholic feelings. H. Quinley and C. Glock in *Anti-Semitism in America* (Macmillan: The Free Press, 1979) provides a readable survey of the pioneering studies of the phenomenon sponsored over the years by the ADL. Also worthy of note is *The Real Anti-Semitism in America* (New York: Arbor House, 1982) by Nathan and Ruth Ann Perlmutter which brings out the newer, less blatant but more "socially acceptable" forms of anti-Semitism (often disguised as anti-Zionism) current in our society today.

In 1979, Judith Hershcopf-Banki of the American Jewish Committee created a controversy which resulted in dialogue, with her report on *Anti-Israel Influences in American Churches.* The study, which dealt mainly with Protestant and Orthodox churches, found "traces of pervasive anti-Jewish polemics" of the past in many recent Christian statements on Israel, a danger we must all work to avoid.

An example of what can be accomplished on the positive side through collaboration is given in Annette Daum and Eugene Fisher, *The Challenge of Shalom for Catholics and Jews,* which provides a discussion guide for joint reflection and action on the 1983 Catholic Bishops' Pastoral on peace and war.

Providing insights into Protestant-Jewish relations in this country is Y. Malachy, *American Fundamentalism and Israel* (Hebrew University of Jerusalem, 1978), which survey the attitudes toward Jews of Jehovah's Witnesses, Pentecostals, Adventists and Dispensationalists.

There has developed a special relationship, not only between American Jews and the State of Israel, but also between American Jews and Christians regarding the State of Israel.

A. James Rudin provides a thorough and enjoyable survey of the broad spectrum of Christian approaches in his *Israel for Christians* (Fortress, 1983), as well as a balanced description of life in Israel today.

David A. Rausch's *Zionism Within Early American Fundamentalism 1878–1918* (Edwin Mellin Press, 1979) provides a glimpse into the precursors of contemporary fundamentalist support for the State of

Israel. This is a book that should be read by those who wish to assess the depth of support and theological motivation of this contemporary phenomenon.

Two works by mainline Christians on Israel deserve serious attention here. Paul M. van Buren's *The Burden of Freedom: Americans and the God of Israel* (Seabury, 1976) is a probing and often profound theological reflection on the meaning of freedom, both human and divine. Van Buren's openness to the continuing validity of Judaism on its own terms provides a basis not only for a critique of traditional Christian theological triumphalism, but also for a fresh vision of Christianity's proper role in Western civilization.

Honor the Promise: America's Commitment to Israel (Doubleday, 1977) by Robert F. Drinan, S.J., is a powerful and deeply moving examination of the need for Christian involvement in the survival of the State of Israel. As priest and congressperson, Drinan analyzes his topic from the theological as well as the political perspective. This magnificent book should be read by all Christians interested in their own history and in the complex world of the Middle East.

Marcus Braybrooke's *Interfaith Organizations 1893–1979* (Edwin Mellin Press, 1980) gives "an historical directory" of a wide range of interreligious institutions and groups. Though he seems much less familiar with Catholic than with Protestant efforts, this will be an invaluable tool for the ecumenical or interreligious officer.

One recent test of Jewish-Christian relations in America occurred in connection with President Reagan's visit to the military cemetery at Bitburg. As Charles E. Silberman noted in *A Certain People: American Jews and Their Lives Today* (N.Y.: Summit), the opposition of Jews to the action of a popular president caused controversy, but no surge of anti-Semitism in the U.S. Geoffrey Hartman has collected pertinent speeches and commentaries in *Bitburg in Moral and Political Perspective* (Indiana University Press, 1986).

8. MISSION AND WITNESS RECONSIDERED

One of the most ancient and disastrous of the tensions between the Jewish and Christian communities has been the problem of proselytism. We have seen how the mere existence of an active, practicing Jewish community worried Chrysostom into a frenzy of invective. "This is the reason I hate the Jews," Chrysostom states, "because they have the Law and the prophets: Indeed I hate them more because of that than if they did not have them." The Jewish scriptures, he complains, are "bait to deceive the simple," and the Law "a snare for the weak" (Wilken, 1983), thus acknowledging the attractiveness of Judaism for Christians and the insecurity of his own faith. It has always been considered by many Christians (especially the insecure) a great prize (at times worth even the most debased and violent tactics, such as forced conversion) to successfully proselytize a Jew.

David Eichhorn, *Evangelizing the American Jew* (Jonathan David, 1978) traces, if superficially, the history of conversionary efforts from Ezra Stiles to today's "Messianic Jews" in this country.

Nor have Jews been slow to defend themselves against over-earnest missionary organizations. A recent American example of a text prepared in self-defense (much as in medieval Europe) can be found in *Jews and Jewish Christianity* by David Berger and Michael Wyschogrod (KTAV, 1978). This is a booklet designed "to persuade Jews who have been attracted by Jewish Christianity to take another look at the issues." Brief and to the point without being polemical, it is of interest to the Christian reader primarily for its glimpse into how the Jewish community reacts to challenges from such conversionary groups as "Jews for Jesus." On this same, highly-charged topic, the essays presented in the Winter 1977 issue of the Anti-Defamation League's *Face to Face,* titled "Christian Mission and Jewish Witness," provide solid historical and theological perspective by major Jewish and Christian thinkers.

Developments in Catholic mission theory since the Second Vatican Council are traced in articles by William Burrows, Paul Knitter, W. Richey Hogg, Thomas Stransky and Eugene Fisher in the January and October, 1985, issues of the *International Bulletin of Missionary Research* (Atlantic City, N.J., Vol. 9, Nos. 1 and 4), along with Evangelical Protestant responses. One of the best single resources on the present state of the debate is Gerald Anderson and Thomas Stransky, eds., *Christ's Lordship and Religious Pluralism* (Maryknoll, N.Y.: Orbis Books, 1981).

Martin A. Cohen and Helga Croner in *Christian Mission-Jewish Mission* (Paulist/Stimulus, 1982) bring together a variety of views (six Christian, two Jewish) on the history and contemporary questions involved in this complex and delicate issue. Crucial to the Catholic view today is the above-mentioned paper by Tommaso Federici (SIDIC, vol. 11:3). Prominent in the discussion, both Catholic and Protestant, is the interpretation of the passage of Matthew 28:19, "Make disciples of all the *ethné* (nations)." Those Christians arguing for conversionary efforts toward the Jews often appeal to this passage as a universal mandate, asking:

"How can we make an exception of the Jews?" Contemporary scholarship, however, would question the exegetical presumption underlying this interpretation, especially since *ethné* should be read in a Jewish context as, properly, *goyim*. Thus, the mandate, in this view, is understood as in the title of an important essay by Daniel Harrington, S.J., and Douglas Hare, "Make Disciples of All the Gentiles" (Catholic Biblical Quarterly 37 [1975] 359–69; reprinted in Daniel Harrington, *Light of All Nations*, Glazier, 1982).

Gerard S. Sloyan's recent survey of the key New Testament passages, "Outreach to Jews and Gentiles" (*Journal of Ecumenical Studies* (Vol. 22:4, Fall 1985) 764–69 concludes that there is no N.T. sanction for "forcing the unwilling to listen to the Gospel" or for any sort of "gentile evangelism" to Jews. "Our God," Sloyan wisely comments "knows how to save who will be saved" (p. 769).

9. TOWARD A CHRISTIAN THEOLOGY OF JUDAISM

Up until the past few years, Christian theological efforts, such as those of Sanders, Moore and Parkes, have concentrated primarily, though not exclusively, on correcting earlier Christian misunderstandings of Judaism. Increasingly, however, attention has turned to the positive side of the picture: What do Christians have to say about themselves and Jews in the light of the now fundamental acknowledgment of the permanent salvific validity of the Jewish covenant for Jews, and of the consequent continuing role of the Jewish people in God's plan of salvation for all humanity? Put more simply, the question is: Once we have removed the polemics against Jews from our theology, what are we left with and what do we put into all those theological "holes" in our teaching? Obviously, such a set of complex questions will not be answered overnight, perhaps not in this generation. But a number of intriguing starts have been made in the last few years.

John Pawlikowski's *What Are They Saying About Christian-Jewish Relations?* (Paulist, 1980) summarizes the range of the dialogue to date in biblical and theological questions and establishes the *status questionis* for future efforts. Pawlikowski updates his survey of theological developments in "New Trends in Catholic Religious Thought" in Fisher, Rudin, Tanenbaum, *Twenty Years* (cf., Section One, above—pp. 169–90). He has in the meantime offered a major contribution of his own in *Christ in the Light of the Christian-Jewish Dialogue* (Paulist, A Stimulus Book, 1982). Here, Pawlikowski offers balanced critiques not only of the christological efforts of those scholars consciously concerned with the dialogue, but also of leading European scholars (Pannenberg, Moltmann, Küng, Schillebeeckx) and Latin American theologians (Gutierrez, Bonino, Sobrino, Boff). Based on the latest scholarship, he offers a refreshingly positive portrait of Jesus' teaching in the light of "its links with and separation from Pharisaic Judaism," and concludes with the beginnings of a christology that can at once establish the uniqueness of the Christ event and yet interpret that event in continuity/discontinuity with creative developments within the evolving rabbinism of the time. As he admits, this is only an initial attempt which needs to be subjected to careful scrutiny by other Christian scholars, but it offers a number of insights of real hope for future work.

Still more recent is Pawlikowski's *Jesus and the Theology of Israel* (Michael Glazier, 1989) mentioned above (Section 2). Pawlikowski clarifies and further develops his earlier work, making this slim volume (99 pages) one of the best single introductions to the field available today.

An initiating, rather than a "finished," document is Clemens Thoma's *A Christian Theology of Judaism* (Paulist, A Stimulus Book, 1980) which attempts an assessment of biblical and systematic theology in the light of what Christians have learned in dialogue with Jews since *Nostra Aetate,* especially regarding "Early and Rabbinic Judaism" (pp. 37–104) and the teaching of Jesus within that context (105–38). The concluding section, "Jews and Christians Since the Time of Christ" presents Thoma's informed views on a variety of historical and theological issues ranging from Christian theories (mostly wrong) concerning early "Jewish Antagonism" toward Christianity to Holocaust Theology and the State of Israel.

A very interesting effort at the systematic renewal of christology can be found in *Who Do You Say I Am? The Christian Understanding of Christ and Antisemitism* by Joseph E. Monti (Paulist, 1984). Monti identifies elements of the religious witness of Jews to Christians: "Judaism reminds Christianity that its faith remains paradoxical, that it is no small matter to speak of the transcending God in such corporeal terms, that its Christology will always be problematic for monotheistic faith, that the messianic reign of peace and justice is not in place, and that Christological triumphalism is out of place amid the horrors of the 20th century inhumanity" (p. 55). Seeking to construct "a non-negating Christology," he reviews the distinction between faith and theology, seeing in "the confusion of confessional fidelity with theological orthodoxy" that followed the adoption of the Chalcedonian formulas, "the basic ground" for the church's historical urge toward sociopolitical conformity that in turn led to the persecution of the Jews. Monti urges "a dialogic Christology," in which the model/analogy for Christian God and Christ-talk will be the human experience of dialogue. As with the efforts of Pawlikowski and Thoma, the effort is a beginning one, framing rather than resolving many essential questions.

Credit for the first full attempt at a truly systematic integration of the implications of the church's contemporary confession of the continuing validity of the covenant between God and the Jewish people, however, must go to Paul M. van Buren's developing masterwork on "A Theology of the Jewish-Christian Reality." The first volume, *Discerning the Way* (Seabury, 1980), initiated the doctrinal conversation by pointing out that all areas of Christian theology are fundamentally affected by this acknowledgment. The second, *A Christian Theology of the People Israel* (Seabury, 1983), undertakes the task itself in classical systematic style. Beginning with clear definitions of the problem and goal facing Christian theology, van Buren then proceeds through considerations of creation, covenant, religious anthropology, evil and hope, election, the people Israel, the Land, Torah, Jesus and Torah, and Jesus and Israel. From the basic point that Israel is "God's elect witness to himself," van Buren then considers, carefully and painstakingly, "The Witness of Israel's Rejection of Christianity," "Israel's Mission," and "The Church's Service to Israel." Throughout this discussion there is a detailed consideration of the writings of St. Paul. The volume should be seen as providing fundamental contributions to the scriptural and missiological discussions surveyed in this report, as well as to systematic theology.

Because it is a pioneering work, there will be, as the author candidly acknowledges in the Foreword, many details and even conclusions which will precipitate strong discussion among van Buren's fellow systematicians. But, given the scope, depth, and clarity of organization of this work, such discussions promise to be fruitful ones whether in the classroom or in academic conferences. Simply put, *A Christian Theology of the People of Israel* should be required reading for all practicing or student Christian theologians today, whatever their fields of specialization.

Van Buren's third volume, *Part III: Christ in Context* (San Francisco: Harper & Row, 1988) concentrates on christology, arguing that Jesus *is* the Christ and Son of God, but *not* the long-awaited Jewish messiah.

Major systematicians, it should be reported, are increasingly turning toward the Christian-Jewish issue and attempting to integrate it, with greater or lesser success, into the overall thrust of their thought. An early example of this effort can be found in the chapter on "The Jewish Question" in Bernard Doering's *Jacques Maritain and the French Catholic Intellectuals* (University of Notre Dame Press, 1983). Many of the themes and insights that eventually went into Vatican II's *Nostra Aetate* and subsequent official Catholic statements are found in the original pioneering work (though not without the flaws of pioneers) of Maritain.

Of great importance to anyone seeking to evaluate the progress of interreligious dialogue since the time of Maritain and Parkes is the question of how the other group is treated in works meant for internal consumption rather than as part of the dialogue process itself. Granted that we tend to say nice things about each other in formal encounters, do such positive insights become integrated into our major theological systems?

Hans Küng's *On Being a Christian* (New York: Doubleday, 1976) is a good test case of this. While Küng's section, which deals specifically with "Christianity and Judaism," is warmly sympathetic and positive, his major approach to christology is somewhat disturbing, at least to the present reviewer. Küng tends to emphasize the uniqueness of Jesus to the point that his Jewishness and his very humanity appear to become questionable. The massive amount of research on the Gospels and on the Pharisees in particular seems to have escaped his purview. And a rather uncritical acceptance of the "Law vs. Gospel" motif of the Reformation finally leads him to a position virtually indistinguishable from old-style polemicism: "It was the Jewish Law that crucified him (Jesus)" (p. 339).

Jürgen Moltmann's *The Church in the Power of the Spirit* (New York: Harper and Row, 1977) is somewhat more successful in integrating Jewish-Christian insight into an overall systematic theology. Moltmann's eschatological perspective enables him to zero in on a central aspect of the current dialogue: the relationship between the Sinai and the Christian covenant(s) in the divine plan for the salvation of humanity. While ambiguities remain in his resolutions, Moltmann does succeed in clarifying the issues that are before us today, especially in his section on Israel (pp. 133–50).

German Catholic theologian Johannes B. Metz's essay, "Christians and Jews After Auschwitz" in *The Emergent Church* (Crossroad, 1981), strikes a deep resonant chord concerning the very way Christians need to do theology today in light of the dialogue when he states that Christians can no longer attempt the theological task alone: "It is possible only together with the victims of Auschwitz. This, in my eyes, is the root of Jewish-Christian Ecumenism" (p. 19).

One excellent example of what Metz is pointing at can be found in Protestant scholar Robert McAfee Brown's theological reflections on *Elie Wiesel: Messenger to All Humanity* (University of Notre Dame, 1983), which argues that it is the very particularity of Jewish peoplehood, and of the Holocaust, that makes possible the universality of Judaism's message. Brown journeys sensitively and compassionately into Wiesel's works (and thus the Kingdom of Darkness) to emerge with a provocative "Revision" of the Christian theological agenda and a certain sense of hope for the future.

An exciting insight into the growing impact of the Holocaust on the developing thought of a major Christian systematician is the essay, "Religious Values after the Holocaust: A Catholic View" by David Tracy in the excellent collection, *Jews and Christians After the Holocaust* edited by Abraham Peck (Fortress, 1982). Here Tracy, who has come to agree with Arthur Cohen that the Holocaust is "theologically the *tremendum* of our age," introduces, in the place of the now-discredited "promise/fulfillment" theology of messianic triumphalism, a more balanced christology which retrieves the eschatological "not yet" for core systematic consideration. Interesting is Tracy's language of "proleptic christology," with its deeply sacramental overtones (such as Rosemary Ruether in the same volume, Gregory Baum in the Fleischner collection, and Monika Hellwig in the Alan T. Davies volume—cf., the scriptural section, above).

Another useful collection of essays that will introduce the reader to the scope of the contemporary dialogue, from questions of scripture, liturgy, and doctrine to those surrounding Christian appreciation of the rebirth of a Jewish State in *Eretz Israel* is found in M. Zeik and M. Siegel, eds., *Root and Branch: The Jewish/Christian Dialogue* (Roth Publishing, 1984). It offers essays by Asher Finkel, Ellis Rivkin, Joseph Grassi, John Pawlikowski, Thomas P. Anderson, James Finn and Gregory Baum, as well as the editors themselves.

A major aspect of Christian reassessment of its stance toward Jewish peoplehood can be evaluated in the extent to which Christian thought comes to grips with the biblical and rabbinic traditions of Land and Covenant. Along with the works of James Parkes, the two most important works by Christians in this field are W.D. Davies' *The Gospel and the Land: Early Christianity and Jewish Territorial Doctrine* (Berkeley: University of California Press, 1974) and W. Bruegemann's, *The Land*

(Fortress, 1977), which centers more on the relationship in the Hebrew scriptures.

Christians will likewise be interested in Lawrence Hoffman, ed., *The Land of Israel: Jewish Perspectives* (University of Notre Dame Press, 1986) covering the biblical Tannaitic, medieval and modern periods.

Two collections of essays, the first in honor of Episcopalian scholar Lee A. Belford of New York University, edited by Norma Thompson and Bruce Cole on *The Future of Jewish-Christian Relations* (Schenectady: Character Research Press, 1982) end this section of our survey of recent literature on the proper note of hope. Presented are essays on the prophets and social justice by Robert Hood and John Kelley, S.M.; on Christian perspectives on the Holocaust by Katherine Hargrove, R.S.C.J., Alice and Roy Eckardt, and Hubert Locke; on tensions arising from mission and liturgy by Paul Kirsch and Cynthia Bronson; on education by Jacob Neusner, Paul Carlson and Hays Rockwell; and on the future of the relationship by Eugene Fisher and Irving Greenberg. The second collection, *Christianity and Judaism: The Deepening Dialogue,* edited by Richard W. Rousseau, S.J. (Ridge Row Press, 1983, cited above), provides one of the best overall surveys of the field now out. Following an excellent "summary synthesis" by the editor, the book contains articles by many of the names referred to in this essay, such as Culbertson, van Buren, Pawlikowski, Fisher, Borowitz, and Williamson, along with trenchant offerings by Rottenberg, Spong, S.T. Davies, H. Siegman, E. Flannery, H. Ditmanson and D. Cairns.

António Barbosa da Silva's *Is There a New Imbalance in the Jewish-Christian Relation?* (Uppsala, Sweden: University of Uppsala, 1985) attempts a "philosophical analysis, from the perspective of the philosophy of religion" (p. 6) of the Christian theologians involved in the dialogue. In fact, da Silva is essentially concerned, from the point of view of his own understanding of the Christian faith, with warning Christian participants that giving in to what he considers to be Jewish "preconditions" for the dialogue will result in the "relativization of Christianity" and the destruction of core Christian beliefs. Despite his good intentions, da Silva does not appear very well-versed in the literature of the dialogue, as described above, or in the official documents of the churches, especially the Catholic Church, since the council. So while some of his comments strike home (e.g., his analyses of the positions of Soloveitchik, pp. 69–70, and Knitter, pp. 100 ff.), his critiques as often as not miss the mark. A major methodological flaw with the effort, in my judgment, is his presumption that Christian-Jewish relations are simply one more form of interreligious relations from the church's point of view. Rather, they are unique. Many of the theological reconsiderations with which da Silva has difficulty (eschewing proselytism, acknowledgment of Jews as God's chosen people today, etc.) stem not from Jewish "preconditions" as he assumes, but rather from internal Christian reflection. They are thus not so easily thrust aside as da Silva would like.

My own response to Christian theological efforts to rethink the relationship between Judaism and Christianity is given in some depth in "Covenant Theology and Jewish-Christian Dialogue," *American Journal of Theology and Philosophy* (Vol. 9, Nos. 1–2, Jan.-May 1988) 5–39.

10. JEWISH RESPONSES TO CHRISTIANITY

On the Jewish side as well there have been responses to the dialogue. For overviews of Jewish reflections on its relations with Christianity, there are two helpful introductory pieces.

Jewish Expressions on Jesus, edited by Trude Weiss-Rosemarin (New York: KTAV, 1977), anthologizes essays spanning several decades of Jewish scholarship from Ben Zion Bokser and Martin Buber to Samuel Sandmel and Solomon Zeitlin. Though marred to some extent by an apologetical undertone, the collection is a valuable library piece. More open in tone and more balanced in the authors selected for scrutiny is Walter Jacob's *Christianity Through Jewish Eyes* (Hebrew Union College Press, KTAV, 1974), which will provide the beginner with an excellent overview of the subject.

An insightful Jewish critique, not so much of the above Christian efforts at renewed christology, as of the earlier work of figures such as Knox, Schoonenberg, Barth, Pannenberg, Rahner, Moltmann and Niebuhr, is Eugene Borowitz' *Contemporary Christologies: A Jewish Response* (Paulist, 1980). Though strongly worded at times, Borowitz' incisiveness consistently helps to clarify what is at stake in the dialogue today.

Helga Croner and Leon Klenicki have edited provocative offerings of major Jewish thinkers in *Issues in the Jewish-Christian Dialogue: Jewish Perspectives on Covenant, Mission and Witness* (Paulist/Stimulus, 1979). In terms of the theological dialogue sketched above, I would single out Manfred Vogel's "Covenant and the Interreligious Encounter" (pp. 62–85) as a marvelously well-balanced Jewish contribution to the essential question of interreligious affirmation of each other's key claims.

Regarding recent Jewish reactions to the figure of Jesus, Pinchas Lapide's *Israelis, Jews and Jesus* (Doubleday, 1979) analyzes the remarkably positive image of Jesus being presented in Israeli textbooks and current thought. Likewise of interest in this category are the works of David Flusser (many of whose essays have been published over the years in *Immanuel* (an English language bulletin published in Jerusalem by the Israel Interfaith Committee) and Geza Vermes' *Jesus the Jew: A Historian's Reading of the Gospels* (Glasgow: Fontana/Collins, 1973). The enduring work of Samuel Sandmel and the developing body of work of Michael Cooke need also to be mentioned here.

Since Sandmel died during the period covered by this essay, I may be permitted in his honor to reflect briefly on some of his lasting contributions to Jewish-Christian understanding (see also Section 2, above). As a Jewish scholar of the New Testament, Sandmel's early works on the Gospels, Philo and St. Paul were remarkable for their objectivity and candor in a period when such qualities were rare. His incisive presidential address, "Parallelomania," delivered at the annual meeting of the Society of Biblical Literature on December 10, 1961, remains a trenchant challenge to all Christian biblical scholars. It is reprinted in a collection of his essays, chiefly from the 1960s, aptly entitled *Two Living Traditions* (Detroit: Wayne State University Press, 1972), a volume which still contains a wealth of fresh insight for those engaged in the dialogue.

In 1965, coinciding with the promulgation of the Second Vatican Council's declaration on the Jews, Sandmel published his *We Jews and Jesus* (Oxford University, 1965, 1973, 1977), which aimed to present the current status of New Testament scholarship primarily to a Jewish audience. In 1967, in the final chapter of *We Jews and You Christians,* he proposed a Jewish counterpart to *Nostra Aetate.* The following selections from that "Proposed Declaration: The Synagogue and the Christian People," I believe, give an insight into Sandmel as scholar and (in the wider sense) ecumenist:

> The Synagogue views the Christian people as among its offspring. It acknowledges that Christian people have laudably spread the message of the Synagogue among people and in areas of the world beyond where the Synagogue had penetrated. . . .

> All men are wont to remember grievances out of which attitudes of vindictiveness arise; therefore the Synagogue reminds its loyal sons of the biblical injunction (Lev. 19:18): "Thou shalt not take vengeance nor bear any grudge against the children of thy people but thou shalt love thy neighbor as thyself." The Synagogue cannot, and does not, hold innocent Christians of our day responsible for the persecutions of

the past, nor all Christians responsible, in the present or the future, for the misdeeds which may come from some.

The Synagogue continues to look forward to that day when all men, of all countries, colors and beliefs, will become spiritually united. Since all universals are attained only through particulars, the Synagogue is committed to the perpetuation of itself against all dissolution. . . . It envisages the unity of humanity in a lofty spiritual bond, enabling men both to preserve the institutions which they hold sacred and to transcend them. (Reprinted in *We Jews and Jesus,* 1977, xv.)

Jewish responses to Christians in dialogue are well summarized and, indeed, substantively carried forward by the great Jewish scholar Jacob Agus in the concluding section (pp. 205–60) of his *The Jewish Quest: Essays on Basic Concepts of Jewish Theology* (New York: KTAV, 1982). The four essays on the New Testament, Israel, the Book of Acts, and Messianism follow up on Agus' earlier work in this field, for example, *Dialogue and Tradition* (New York: Abelard-Schuman, 1971).

David Novak has more recently attempted a thorough development of theory from the Jewish side in *Jewish-Christian Dialogue: A Jewish Justification* (Oxford University Press, 1989). Novak analyzes the rabbinic doctrine of the Noahide Laws as these applied to Gentiles, the medieval Jewish openings to Christianity (e.g., Meiri, Maimonides), and more recent attempts such as those of Martin Buber and Franz Rosenzweig as the basis for his very solid "New Theology of Jewish-Christian Dialogue."

Another exciting theoretical work on the relationship between Judaism and Christianity from the Jewish side now being done is that of Irving Greenberg, whose essay envisioning an "Organic Model" of the relationship between the faiths is found in Fisher, Rudin, Tanenbaum, *Twenty Years* (Paulist, pp. 191–211).

Two recent major works, also by Orthodox Jewish theologians, should engage the direct attention of Christian systematicians. Pinchas Lapide's *The Resurrection of Jesus: A Jewish Perspective* (Augsburg, 1983) accepts the resurrection of Jesus as an "historical event," though he does not, of course, accept the high christological interpretation of that event which is definitive for Christians. Michael Wyschogrod's *The Body of Faith: Judaism as Corporeal Election* (Seabury, 1983) discusses Jewish self-understanding in "incarnational" terms, though not on the level of an individual Jew (Jesus) but on that of God's indwelling in the whole people Israel. While not primarily oriented to the dialogue, Wyschogrod's effort illustrates the mutuality of dialogue, properly understood.

Finally, in this section on Jewish responses to Christianity, mention should be made of the "analysis and critique" by a Christian of Jewish scholars who have sought, from within Jewish tradition, to frame a positive reappraisal of the figure of Jesus. Donald A. Hagner's *The Jewish Reclamation of Jesus* (Grand Rapids: Zondervan, 1984) is written from a confessionally Evangelical point of view, often using Christian faith perspectives as criteria in judging the "adequacy of Jewish scholarship."

Hagner perceptively notes the existence of certain "patterns" among Jewish scholars who have written on Jesus in his first-century Jewish context. In summarizing this growing literature, the volume will be quite useful for Christian readers. Hagner effectively critiques what he aptly calls the *nihil novi* dictum of most Jewish scholars, i.e., "what is good in the Gospels is nothing new; what is new is nothing good," though he strains, at times to find "originality" in Jesus' teaching.

Hagner's central criticism, however, is that Jewish scholars do not accept basic Christian claims *about* Jesus (e.g., Jesus' unique authority as a teacher, his messiahship, etc.). Hagner is correct in this. But one wonders why he feels the need to belabor so obvious a point, or why he would expect Jews to accept Christian theological interpretations of the Christ event in their work. A certain recurring polemical attitude toward what are, after all, sincere and often helpful contributions to our understanding of the historical Jesus mars what otherwise might have been a helpful contribution.

11. LITURGY, SPIRITUALITY AND CATECHETICS

The increasing awareness of Christian dependency on Jewish spirituality for its own liturgical forms of worship deserves special treatment in this essay. Whereas earlier efforts tended to feature Christians writing about their "debt to Israel" in this context, more recent works have taken on a more dialogical tone.

Three still helpful examples of the former approach can be found in the following:

The Spirituality of Judaism (Abbey Press, 1977) is designed as a serious introduction to its topic for the non-specialist. Three prominent French Catholic theologians (Roger Le Deaut, Annie Jaubert and Kurt

Hruby) present the history and dynamics of Jewish spirituality in a well-written, concise fashion.

Second, William Simpson's *Light and Rejoicing* (Belfast: Christian Journals, 1976) provides a down-to-earth introduction to Jewish worship for the average Christian. A Methodist minister, Simpson is international secretary for the Council of Christians and Jews.

Third, special issues of SIDIC on "Jewish and Christian Liturgy" (Vol. 6, 1973) and "Aspects of Jewish and Christian Prayer" (Vol. 8, 1975), as well as occasional related titles (Vol. 10, 1977, "Sabbath and Sunday") have chronicled the development of thought in this rich area of dialogical retrieval. In this category also belong two earlier classics: L. Bouyer's "Jewish and Christian Liturgies," in L. Sheppard, ed., *True Worship* (Helicon Press, 1963) and, from the Jewish side, Eric Werner's *The Sacred Bridge* (Schocken, 1970). Werner's second volume (N.Y.: KTAV, 1984), focuses on "the interdependence of liturgy and music in synagogue and church in the first millennium."

Of more recent vintage are two collections which involve Jewish and Christian scholars working together. First, Asher Finkel and Lawrence Frizzell, in honor of Msgr. John Oesterreicher of Seton Hall University, have co-edited *Standing Before God: Studies on Prayer in Scripture and Tradition* (KTAV, 1981). This brings together twenty-six articles, many of surpassing importance for the dialogue, such as Gerard Sloyan's "Who Are the People of God?" (pp. 102–116). D. Zeller's "God as Father" (117–129) and Asher Finkel's "The Prayer of Jesus in Matthew" (131–170) develop insights on the much-misunderstood "Abba, Father" phrase first introduced by John Oesterreicher in J. Petuchowski and M. Brocke, eds., *The Lord's Prayer and Jewish Liturgy* (Seabury Crossroad, 1978). This latter volume includes an especially well-selected collection of essays presenting Jewish spirituality at the time of Jesus and, by extension, offering a unique insight into Jesus' own form of prayer, especially, of course, the Our Father, which emerges with greater depth as its essential Jewishness is unfolded.

Eugene J. Fisher surveys developments in Catholic liturgical tradition in "The Roman Liturgy and Catholic-Jewish Relations" in Fisher, Rudin, Tanenbaum, *Twenty Years* (cf. Section one, above—pp. 135–155).

A major new publication synthesizes much of the earlier work and adds a significant contribution of its own. Leon Klenicki and Gabe Huck in *Spirituality and Prayer: Jewish and Christian Understandings* (Paulist,

Stimulus, 1983) have collected eight articles by Christian and Jewish scholars on various liturgical topics. A unique feature of the book is Joseph Gutmann's "Christian Influences on Jewish Customs," one of the few studies of the "other side of the interrelational coin" ever published. This latter approach is one that deserves much greater attention on the part of Jewish scholars. Two millennia of living together with Christians, albeit at times uneasily, cannot but have left a deeper mark on rabbinic spiritual tradition than one might at first wish to acknowledge.

Pinchas Lapide's *Hebrew in the Church* (Grand Rapids: Eerdmans, 1984) is a marvelous contribution that is difficult to classify. In it, the emminent Israeli scholar catalogs the various efforts by Christians to put the New Testament and Christian liturgy into Hebrew, some of them with conversionist intent. His analysis of the difficulties faced by these efforts is both fascinating and important for an understanding of the dialogue today.

Since liturgy, to be done well, must be coordinated with solid cate-chetical formation, a few examples of materials for teachers may properly be included here. Recommended, again, is *SIDIC,* which specializes in materials for teachers, such as the recent issue on the Vatican "Notes on Preaching and Catechesis" (Vol. 19. no. 2, 1986).

Claire Huchet Bishop's *How Catholics Look at Jews* (New York: Paulist, 1974) does for European Catholic textbooks what J. Pawli-kowski's earlier report (*Catechetics and Prejudice,* Paulist, 1973) did for pre-Vatican II American texts; namely, it summarizes in readable style the findings of studies of the treatment of Jews and Judaism in Catholic teaching materials. Together with my own update of the studies described by Pawlikowski (see *Faith Without Prejudice,* Ch. 7), these inexpensive paperbacks give a clear and often surprising analysis of how we describe (and all too often stereotype) Jews in our classrooms and from our pulpits.

These Catholic studies, of course, owe much to the pioneering work of Protestant scholar Bernard Olson, whose classic *Faith and Prejudice* (Yale University, 1963) virtually created the field in this country. Olson's work was updated by Gerald Strober in *Portrait of an Elder Brother* (American Jewish Committee, 1972).

Solid, popular-level books by Christians on Judaism are also appearing in increasing numbers, many issued in paperback. Among the best is *Sinai and Calvary* by John Pawlikowski (Benzinger, 1976). Both readable and reflecting the best of modern scholarship in its summary of Jewish history and Jewish-Christian relations, this book is eminently suited to high school and adult groups. Paul Carlson's *O Christian! O Jew!* (David C. Cook, 1974) while not as thorough as Pawlikowski's, is nonetheless most readable and remarkable for its sensitivity.

Homework for Christians Preparing for Jewish-Christian Dialogue (National Conference of Christians and Jews, 1986) by Eugene Fisher is aimed at a general audience (upper-level high school, college, adult). It is set up for use in a discussion group of six (or fewer) sessions. With readings and discussion questions for each section, it introduces the reader to the basics of the history and contemporary reality of the dialogue. Rabbi Edward Zerin's *What Catholics and Other Christians Should Know About Jews* (Wm. C. Brown, 1980) is a solid introductory test for high school students. A similar effort, written for adults, is Rabbi Stuart E. Rosenberg's *Christians and Jews: the Eternal Bond* (New York: Frederick Ungar, 1985). Both can be highly recommended, as can Leon Klenicki and Geoffrey Wigoder's handy *A Dictionary of the Jewish-Christian Dialogue* (Paulist, A Stimulus Book, 1984).

The Anti-Defamation League of B'nai B'rith (ADL) and the Secretariat for Catholic-Jewish Relations of the National Conference of Catholic Bishops have jointly sponsored a limited publication of *Abraham, Our Father in Faith,* a religion teacher's curriculum guide. This guide, developed originally by the Archdiocese of Philadelphia, has been sent to all diocesan school superintendents and to ADL regional directors as an aid in integrating Catholic-Jewish understandings in the curriculum from pre-school through grade 12. The booklet forms a companion piece to the teacher-training program, *Understanding the Jewish Experience* (ADL/ United States Catholic Conference, 1979), co-authored by E. Fisher and L. Klenicki.

Also co-authored by Fisher and Klenicki is a series of articles and curriculum guides on "Basic Jewish and Christian Beliefs in Dialogue," designed for classroom use. Included, along with treatment of doctrinal issues such as Creation, Sin, the Kingdom and Covenant, are curricula for course segments on "Preparing for the Dialogue" and "Antisemitism" (published in PACE, Professional Approaches for Christian Educators, St. Mary's Press, Winona, MN 55987: 1982–84). These have recently been put together as a single text for educators by the ADL and are being translated into Spanish by the Latin American Bishops' Conference (CELAM) for distribution throughout Central and South America.

A contemporary liturgy might also be mentioned here for those readers interested in having Seders in their parishes. Leon Klenicki's *The Passover Celebration,* published jointly by the ADL and Archdiocese of

Chicago (May, 1980) fills a long felt need. Also helpful in this regard are the guidelines for Seder meals for Christians, put out by the Archdiocese of Louisville, in April, 1979.

Two books, both by Christians, discuss the relationship between Passover and eucharist in some detail. Anthony J. Saldarini's *Jesus and Passover* (Paulist, 1984) provides an excellent, well-balanced survey of the key relationships from a Catholic biblical and liturgical point of view. This book, which does not omit discussion of the continuing development of the Passover ritual in Jewish tradition after the first century provides the most solid and useful introduction of the various issues to date. Gillian Feeley-Harnik's *The Lord's Table: Eucharist and Passover in Early Christianity* (University of Pennsylvania Press, 1981) is more speculative, offering an anthropological study of the symbolic meaning of the Passover ritual as adapted by the early Christian community to its own understandings of the Christ event. Given the central position of food in Jewish ritual life, she argues, it was natural for the early Church to structure not only the eucharist but also the Gospel narratives of the Passion itself around the elements of the traditional Seder.

Another anthropological approach to Passover, this time from a purely Jewish perspective, can be found in Ruth Gruber Fredman's *The Passover Seder: Afikoman in Exile* (University of Pennsylvania Press, 1981), which traces through the constantly enriching development of the ritual's symbolic elements, how the Seder continues to be an essential part of the process by which Jewish society creates and defines itself anew "throughout the generations" (Ex 12:16).

Distilling the liturgical issues into an official church document is *God's Mercy Endures Forever: Guidelines on the Presentation of Jews and Judaism in Catholic Preaching* (National Conference of Catholic Bishops, Washington, D.C., 1988), which offers assistance for homilists throughout the liturgical year.

As a transition to the next section, an earlier publication of the Stimulus Foundation may be cited. This is: *From Death to Hope: Liturgical Reflections on the Holocaust,* a Yom Hashoah service for Christians and Jews, written by E. Fisher and L. Klenicki. It has been included as well in *The Six Days of Destruction* (N.Y.: Paulist, 1988) by Elie Wiesel and Albert Friedlander. A new edition was published in 1990 by Liturgical Training Publications, Archdiocese of Chicago.

12. THE HOLOCAUST AND CHRISTIAN-JEWISH RELATIONS

a. The Righteous Among the Nations

Five works, four of them by Jewish authors, give testimony to the heroism of Christians who risked their lives to save Jews. The most exciting and dramatic of these accounts is Alexander Ramati's *The Assisi Underground: Priests Who Rescued Jews* (Stein and Day, 1978), which tells of the clandestine forging of papers for Jews and suspense-filled escapes, all sponsored by the local bishops and run from the monasteries and convents of the city of St. Francis. P. Hallie's *Lest Innocent Blood Be Shed* (Harper and Row, 1979) tells of a small French Protestant village which organized non-violently to harbor Jews. Philip Friedman's *Their Brother's Keepers* (Holocaust Library, 1978) narrates many inspiring stories of Christian heroism during World War II, and remains the most complete overall collection of such incidents. Peter Hellman's *Avenue of the Righteous* provides moving portraits of four heroic Christians and of the Jews they saved from Hitler. Finally, Harvey Rosenfeld's *Raoul Wallenberg: Angel of Rescue* (Prometheus, 1982) recounts the dramatic story of the young Swedish diplomat who snatched hundreds of Jews from the death camps of Adolf Eichmann. Rosenfeld also records the efforts of the papal nuncio in Hungary, Bishop Angelo Rotta, and his aide, Tibor Baranski, to help baptised and unbaptised Jews alike, especially in the last, critical years of 1944–45.

Included among the righteous Christians would have to be those millions, including thousands of Christian clergy who, for various reasons, were also martyred by the Nazi death machine. B. Wytwycky's *The Other Holocaust* (The Novak Report, 1980) tells this story admirably, and without any sense of attempting thereby to diminish the uniqueness of the Jewish tragedy.

Thomas Kenneally's story of the efforts of the German Catholic industrialist Oskar Schindler, who risked his life and spent his fortune to protect Jews, is both highly readable as a novel and highly informative as history. *Schindler's List* (Simon and Schuster, 1982), Penguin Books, 1983), which is based on the testimony of numerous *Schindlerjuden,* provides perhaps the most complete portrait of a "righteous Gentile" in the literature.

Nechama Tec's *When Light Pierced the Darkness* (Oxford University Press, 1986) focuses on Polish Catholics who saved Jewish lives, offering a new theory of altruistic behavior. Christians who helped, she concludes, helped not just friends, but more often strangers and even people they disliked.

b. The Church and the Holocaust

Father John Morley's *Vatican Diplomacy and the Jews During the Holocaust 1939-1943* (KTAV, 1980) analyzes Vatican records of efforts to aid Jews. While Morley cites numerous interventions by Vatican officials to oppose Nazi racial legislation and the deportation of Jews to the death camps, his final conclusion is that more could have been done. For the years 1944-45 (not covered by the Morley book), Robert A. Graham, S.J., provides significant background in his monograph, "Pius XII's Defense of Jews and others: 1944-45" (Catholic League for Religious and Civil Rights, 1982) with an introduction by Joseph Lichten of ADL. Graham has edited the twelve-volume set of documents on the activities of the Vatican Secretariat of State during World War II, a rich source as yet untapped by most scholars in the field, with the notable exception of Morley.

E.C. Helmreich's scholarly *The German Churches Under Hitler* (Wayne State University Press, 1979) portrays the church struggle, both Catholic and Protestant, with Nazi domination. Paired with this should be the collection of papers given at the 1970 International Scholars conference on *The German Church Struggle and the Holocaust,* edited by Franklin Littel and Hubert Locke (Wayne State University Press, 1974). Of particular interest for Catholics is Gordon Zahn's article, "Catholic Resistance?"

On the latter theme, Wayne State University has also put out G. Lewy's *The Catholic Church and Nazi Germany* (1974), and Gordon Zahn has produced a dramatic analysis in *German Catholics and Hitler's Wars* (Sheed and Ward, 1962). Zahn, while concentrating on why there was so little conscientious objection among German Catholics, helps to underscore the mind-set of the times. Very important for understanding the reactions to Nazism on the part of church officials is Anthony Rhodes' highly readable *The Vatican in the Age of the Dictators 1922-1945* (Holt, Rinehart, Winston, 1973), which should be required reading for anyone trying to piece together the reasons why people did what they did during those troubled times.

Of equal interest to what the churches did (and failed to do) during the Holocaust is the question of how Christian theology has reacted to it since the war. Has it become, as for Tracy and Cohen, a theological *tremendum* precipitating the necessary fundamental revision of Christian thought to prevent its recurrence? Or will it become a small footnote? Much of the answer (on which, I believe, the continuing integrity of the Christian theological enterprise depends), has been given in section 9, above. The appearance in the last few years of so many "After Auschwitz" collections and essays by Christians as well as Jews, as compared with the thundering silence on the subject that perdured in Christian journals and texts from World War II up until the early 1970s gives one measure that at least a beginning has been made in taking up this crucial challenge that faces all Christians. In this sense, it can be said that the Jewish-Christian reality, since it reflects the most ancient of Christian schisms and heresies, retains a "theological priority" on the ecumenical agenda. In addition to the works listed in the "Christian Theology" section, I would recommend the following:

Eva Fleischner's *Judaism in German Christian Theology Since 1945* (Scarecrow, 1975) shows that the anti-Semitic obsession was equally embedded in the highest levels of German scholarship both before and after the war. Given the influence of German theologians on American theological training, this should give us pause to reflect on our own seminary training and its adequacy today.

For handy summaries of the range of Christian (and Jewish) thought reacting theologically to the Holocaust today, there are two brief articles: Alice Eckardt's "The Holocaust: Christian and Jewish Responses" (*Journal of the American Academy of Religion,* Sept. 1974) and E. Fisher, "Ani Ma'amin: Directions in Holocaust Theology" (*Interface,* Secretariat for Catholic-Jewish Relations, National Conference of Catholic Bishops, Winter, 1980). A fuller and highly stimulating survey of the issues can be found in J. Pawlikowski's *The Challenge of the Holocaust for Christian Theology* (ADL, 1980) and in his above-mentioned *What Are They Saying. . . ?*

Haim Genizi's *American Apathy: The Plight of Christian Refugees from Nazism* (Ramat-Gan, Israel: Bar-Ilan University, 1983) places the indifference of Americans toward Jewish refugees in the context of their overall apathy toward the victims of Nazism.

The slow awakening of concern shown by the Catholic and Protestant communities to the plight of their own co-religionists, and their difficulties in developing effective relief agencies for them, is a fascinating and hitherto untold story. Genizi corrects several commonly-held misperceptions of the period showing, for example, the dramatic effect of

Pius XI's condemnation of Nazism (*Mit Brennender Sorge,* 1937) in galvanizing American Catholic protests against Hitler, and the tireless efforts of the Apostolic Delegate in Washington, Amleto Cicognani, "to save as many Jews as the situation enabled" (p. 165). It was not until toward the end of the war, however, that the U.S. Catholic relief agencies began to match the Protestants (especially Quakers) in organizational effectiveness.

David S. Wyman's *The Abandonment of the Jews* (New York: Pantheon, 1984) focuses primarily on American governmental actions (or, rather, inactions) to assist Jews, such as those of the State Department and the War Refugee Board. The portrait is often devastating, and should serve to caution those who would honor American behavior at the expense of European efforts.

Two personal responses to the Holocaust, one by a Catholic, the other by an Episcopalian priest, give moving testimony to the anguish of the Christian conscience which confronts honestly the fact of massive Christian complicity in and silence during the Holocaust. Harry James Cargas' *A Christian Response to the Holocaust* (Stonehenge, 1981) is a moving plea for Christians to open their hearts to the implications of the absolute evil set free in the midst of supposedly "Christian" Europe. "The failure of Christianity in the mid-20th century is monumental," Cargas writes—"is it fatal?" Alan Ecclestone's *The Night Sky of the Lord* (Schocken, 1982) is an eloquent, often poetic and deeply spiritual meditation. The Holocaust, and Christian involvement in it have prompted Ecclestone to search back through the whole grisly history of Christian anti-Semitism to probe how such monstrous evil could have come about.

Also prompted to search into Christian history through confrontation with the Holocaust was Malcolm Hay, the eminent Catholic historian. Hay's research, always well-balanced and professional, produced the book, *Foot of Pride,* first published in this country some three decades ago. Hay brings to his writing the wry wit and sense for the ironic of the Scot that he was. It is an occasion for gratitude that ADL has brought this great Catholic classic out in a new edition, with excellent introductions prepared especially for the edition by Claire Huchet Bishop and Edward Flannery, under the title *The Roots of Christian Anti-Semitism* (ADL Freedom Library, 1981).

Likewise deserving special mention here, is the reissuance of Edward Flannery's *The Anguish of the Jews* (Paulist, Stimulus 1985), which substantially revises and updates the earlier classic. One can perceive in

Flannery's modifications of previous conclusions the increasing openness of Christians to acknowledging just how deeply embedded anti-Semitism has become in Christian thought over the centuries.

A. Roy Eckardt, writing with his wife, Alice, has graced the field with a new and challenging work, *Long Night's Journey into Day: Life and Faith after the Holocaust* (Detroit: Wayne State University Press, 1982). The Eckardts probe both history and contemporary theology not only for answers but also to clarify the proper questions to be asked, analyzing the responses of selected modern theologians and church councils. They conclude that after the Holocaust it is no longer sufficient for Christian theology to continue to fall back on the events of Crucifixion-Resurrection-Parousia as solely decisive for Christian doctrine's response to the ultimate horror of the demonic.

There are several recent collections of essays on the Holocaust which are worthy of note. Michael D. Ryan, ed. *Human Responses to the Holocaust* brings together the papers of the National Conference of Christians and Jews' 1979 Bernard E. Olson Symposium on the Church Struggle and the Holocaust (New York: Edwin Mellin Press, 1981). The collection includes descriptions of the operation of the death camps, survivors' testimonies, Christian resistance in the Netherlands, Denmark and Germany, and theological articles on messianism by Robert McAfee Brown and Jacob Agus.

O.D. Kulka and P.R. Mendes-Flohr have provided a real service to the field by editing the volume, *Judaism and Christianity Under the Impact of National Socialism,* for The Historical Society of Israel (Jerusalem, 1987). It contains fine essays on a country-by-country basis, as well as helpful discussions for the contemporary encounter by Arthur Cohen, Marcel Dubois, Franklin Littell and Zwi Werblowsky.

H. Friedlander and S. Milton, eds. *The Holocaust: Ideology, Bureaucracy and Genocide* (Kraus International Publications, 1981) collect the papers of two NCCJ Conferences held in San José, CA. Treated are the history of anti-Semitism in Europe and in Weimar Germany, the professions (law, medicine, the physical sciences, technology, government, the churches, and other intellectual studies) and how they were co-opted into participation in the genocide, and theological reflections by Franklin Littell, Paul van Buren, and John Pawlikowski. H. Friedlander's concluding essay on methodology for teaching about the Holocaust provides an excellent introduction for educators.

I. Shur, F. Littell, and M. Wolfgang, eds. *Reflections on the Holo-*

caust: Historical, Philosophical, Educational is a special issue of *The Annals* of the American Academy of Political and Social Sciences (Vol. 450, July, 1980). Included in it are treatments of the Jewish-Christian implications by the Eckardts, John S. Conway, Robert F. Drinan, and Franklin Littell. The addition of a thorough index makes this one of the most usable of essay collections.

Another special issue, this time of the *Journal of Ecumenical Studies* (Winter, 1981), documents a fascinating "Jewish-Christian Dialogue between Americans and Germans" which followed a year-long exchange of papers between students and faculty of Temple University, Philadelphia, and several German universities. The exchange is a rich and heartening record of what G.D. Earley calls "The Radical Hermeneutical Shift in Post-Holocaust Christian Thought."

The October, 1984, volume of the Concilium series, edited by Elizabeth Schüssler Fiorenza and David Tracy probes *The Holocaust as Interruption: A Question for Christian Theology,* with articles by Arthur Cohen, J.B. Metz, John Pawlikowski and others.

Numerous helpful teacher resources on the Holocaust are also available today. The Anti-Defamation League (ADL, 823 United Nations Plaza, New York, NY 10017) and the American Jewish Committee (AJC, 165 E. 56th St., New York, NY 10022) both have available a wealth of written and audio-visual materials. ADL's interreligious bulletin, *Face to Face,* has come out with special issues which provide solid background on the Holocaust (Spring, 1979; Winter, 1981). ADL also puts out a unique, newspaper-format teaching tool called "The Record," which is excellent for classroom use, as well as a model curriculum by Ann L. Nick, *Teachers' Guide to the Holocaust* and many other teacher resources. AJC has two booklets useful in a variety of programs: *The Many Faces of Antisemitism* and *About the Holocaust: What We Know and How We Know It.*

Two annotated bibliographies by Catholics will be extremely helpful in discovering educational resources: Eva Fleischner, "Select Annotated Bibliography" (Horizons, Spring, 1977), and H. J. Cargas, *The Holocaust* (Catholic Library Association, 461 W. Lancaster, Haverford, PA 19041). The latter has been updated by Lawrence Frizzell of Seton Hall University (South Orange, NJ 07079).

For a summary of anti-Semitic events throughout the ages leading to the Holocaust, and subsequent to it up to 1982, Paul Grosser and Edwin Halperin's *Anti-Semitism: Causes and Effects* (New York: Philosophical

Library, 1983) is quite useful. Its "Catalogue of Anti-Semitic Events" beginning with the fall of the temple focuses primarily on Christian acts against Jews (pp. 49–236) though a brief chronology of anti-Jewish events under Islam (pp. 383–419) is appended.

Other surveys are Shumel Almag, ed. *Antisemitism Through the Ages* (Oxford: Pergamon Press, 1988) and *Persistent Prejudice* (Fairfax, VA: George Mason Univ. Press, 1988), edited by H. Hirsch and J. Spiro. My own analysis of the evolving literature in this field is included in the opening essay of the latter volume: "Anti-Semitism and Christianity: Theories and Revisions of Theories" (pp. 11–30).

13. MUSLIM-JEWISH-CHRISTIAN RELATIONS

Recently, the experience of "trialogue" (a neologism, but then, a new reality as well) between the three great monotheistic religions has begun to be explored. Ignaz Maybaum's *Trialogue Between Jew, Christian and Muslim* (London: Routledge & Kegan, 1973) presents the thinking of the German-Jewish philosopher Franz Rosenzweig as a starting point for today. Maybaum's style, however, is definitely not for beginners.

More dynamically, the Interreligious Peace Colloquium (now the Muslim-Jewish-Christian Conference) begun by Monsignor Joseph Gremillion as "a movement for international peace, justice and human rights" has initiated major programs to bring representatives of the three faiths together. *World Faiths and the New World Order* (MJCC, 3700 Thirteenth Street, N.E., Washington, D.C. 20017) contains the proceedings of a conference held in Lisbon, Portugal in November of 1977. This was followed by the "Harvard Seminar on Faith Communities as Transnational Actors" (March, 1979), and a major session held at the AAR/ SBL meeting in New York which featured the late Cardinal Pignedoli of the Vatican (*Origins*, Vol. 9, p. 516).

The papers from the American Academy of Religion Colloquium have been edited by Isma'il al Faruqi in *Trialogue of the Abrahamic Faiths* (International Institute of Islamic Thought, 1982). A scholar from each tradition addresses three topics: How each perceives the other two traditions in relation to their own; "The Nation State as a Form of Social Organization," and "The Faith Community as Transnational Actor for Justice and Peace."

The Kennedy Institute for Ethics at Georgetown University is sponsoring perhaps the most unique, ongoing dialogue of Jewish, Christian, and Muslim scholars in the world today. Its founding goals have been published in *SIDIC* (Vol. 12:3, 1979) and a summary of its first four years of discussion in the *Journal of Ecumenical Studies* (Winter, 1982). The papers of an earlier effort hosted by Graymoor Ecumenical Institute were published in a special issue of the *Journal of Ecumenical Studies* in the Summer of 1977. My own reflection on the Kennedy Institute dialogue and on possibilities for the future are contained in "In the Name of the One God: Jewish, Christian, Muslim Trialogue," *PACE 16* (St. Mary's Press, 1986) 179–82.

Muslim-Christian and Muslim-Jewish relations are also underway. For background in the former, a special issue of the *Pro Mundi Vita* bulletin (September, 1978) summarizes the last ten years of dialogue. *We Believe in One God,* edited by A. Schimmel and A. Falaturi (Seabury, 1979) contains articles by Muslims and Christians on themes such as Jesus and Muhammed, revelation, history and creation. *Islamochristiana* is a journal devoted to Catholic-Muslim issues, published by the Pontifical Institute of Arabic Studies in Rome. An insightful selection of essays can be found in Richard W. Rousseau, S.J., ed. *Christianity and Islam: The Struggling Dialogue* (Scranton: Ridge Row Press, 1985).

The most informative background work to date on the historical and interreligious development of the three monotheistic traditions is to be found in F.E. Peters' *Children of Abraham: Judaism/Christianity/Islam* (Princeton University Press, 1982). Peters' works systematically through, first, the historical origins of each community and, then, their developing attitudes toward and practices of such essential elements of religious communal life as: community and hierarchy, law, scripture and tradition, liturgy, asceticism and mysticism, theology and sacred history. Peters' approach enables him to highlight the interrelatedness of the three traditions without losing sight of the uniqueness of each. His attention to political and sociological consequences of the reactions of each community to similar challenges (e.g., gnosticism and Hellenistic philosophy) enables him to present a much more dynamic understanding than is usually gained in typical comparative religion texts.

Bat Ye'or's *The Dhimmi: Jews and Christians Under Islam* (Fairleigh Dickinson University Press, 1985) presents the negative side of Muslim treatment of "the peoples of the book." Its extensive documentation (pp. 161–405) makes it a useful reference tool.

For beginners, Edward W. Bauman's *Children of Abraham* (Bauman

Bible Telecasts, 1981), which is actually a study guide for a T.V. course, interweaves brief descriptions of the beliefs of each of the three traditions on central topics such as God, faith, scripture, worship, and justice, with selected readings from the sacred texts.

The literature on Muslim-Jewish relations over the centuries is large. ADL's *Bibliographic Essays in Medieval Jewish Studies* (KTAV, 1976) has an excellent section on this history. N. Stillman's *The Jews of Arab Lands* (Jewish Publication Society, 1979) gives both an engrossing account of that history and a number of basic sources in translation, and is now being updated to include more contemporary material.

An interesting experiment in Jewish-Christian-Muslim encounter has been conducted over the past few years by Haim Gordon of Ben Gurion University of Negev, Beersheva, Israel. Gordon has formed what he calls three traditions in the art of dialogue following the principles of Martin Buber. He has achieved both interesting success, and has encountered real difficulties as well. Reports on his pioneering efforts can be found in the journal, *Teachers College Record 82* (no. 2, Winter, 1980, 211–310), *84* (no. 1, Fall 1982, 210–25), and *85* (no. 1, Fall 1983, 73–87), with a critical and constructive response by Muslim scholar Riffat Hassanin in *TCR 84* (no. 1, Fall, 1982, 226–31).

Anyone organizing or going on a tour of Israel will welcome the following: Jerome Murphy O'Conner, *The Holy Land, An Archaeological Guide from Earlier Times to 1700* (Oxford University, 1980), and Franklin Littell, *A Pilgrim's Interfaith Guide to the Holy Land* (Carta and Jerusalem Post, 1981). The latter has the unusual feature of a glossary of the people for whom streets and other places have been named in Israel, which will make wandering the streets of Jerusalem an even more pleasurable adventure. For those interested in a more thorough, though still quite readable. archaeological survey, I would recommend Yohanan Aharoni's *The Archaeology of the Land of Israel* (Westminster Press). Aharoni concentrates on Israelite life from the prehistoric period through the fall of the first temple.

CONCLUSION

In summary, it must be said that perhaps never before in history have two great world religions engaged themselves with each other so productively in so short a time. This bibliography, while not brief, has been exemplary rather than exhaustive, and limited in the main to works in the English language. There exists here a burgeoning, indeed exploding, body of literature, as if the pent-up energies of two millennia are finally being released. In all of this one can only discern, humbly and hesitatingly, the hand of the One God, the God of Abraham, Isaac and Jacob, of Sarah, Rivkah and Rachel, the One God of Israel and of the Christian Church.

other volumes in this series

Stepping Stones to Further Jewish-Christian Relations: An Unabridged Collection of Christian Documents, compiled by Helga Croner (A Stimulus Book, 1977).

Helga Croner and Leon Klenicki, editors, *Issues in the Jewish-Christian Dialogue: Jewish Perspectives on Covenant, Mission and Witness* (A Stimulus Book, 1979).

Clemens Thoma, *A Christian Theology of Judaism* (A Stimulus Book, 1980).

Helga Croner, Leon Klenicki and Lawrence Boadt, C.S.P., editors, *Biblical Studies: Meeting Ground of Jews and Christians* (A Stimulus Book, 1980).

John T. Pawlikowski, O.S.M., *Christ in the Light of the Christian-Jewish Dialogue* (A Stimulus Book, 1982).

Martin Cohen and Helga Croner, editors, *Christian Mission-Jewish Mission* (A Stimulus Book, 1982).

Leon Klenicki and Gabe Huck, editors, *Spirituality and Prayer: Jewish and Christian Understandings* (A Stimulus Book, 1983).

• Leon Klenicki and Geoffrey Wigoder, editors, *A Dictionary of the Jewish-Christian Dialogue* (A Stimulus Book, 1984).

Edward Flannery, *The Anguish of the Jews* (A Stimulus Book, 1985).

More Stepping Stones to Jewish-Christian Relations: An Unabridged Collection of Christian Documents 1975–1983, compiled by Helga Croner (A Stimulus Book, 1985).

Clemens Thoma and Michael Wyschogrod, editors, *Understanding Scripture: Explorations of Jewish and Christian Traditions of Interpretation* (A Stimulus Book, 1987).

Bernard J. Lee, S.M., *The Galilean Jewishness of Jesus* (A Stimulus Book, 1988).

Clemens Thoma and Michael Wyschogrod, editors, *Parable and Story in Judaism and Christianity* (A Stimulus Book, 1989).